Understanding the Mystery of the Mass

Si Scires Donum Dei

Reflections on the Mass by Father Matthew Buettner

Foreword by
Dr. Alice von Hildebrand

Queenship

PUBLISHING COMPANY
P.O. Box 220 • Goleta, CA 93116
800-647-9882 • 805-692-0043 • Fax 805-967-5133
www.queenship.org

Nihil Obstat:
Reverend Giles Dimock, O.P., S.T.D.
Adjunct Faculty; Franciscan University of Steubenville
9 July 2005

Imprimatur:
Most Reverend Peter J. Jugis, J.C.D.
Bishop of Charlotte
15 August 2005
Solemnity of the Assumption of the Blessed Virgin Mary

Library of Congress Number #2006901038

Published by:
Queenship Publishing
P.O. Box 220
Goleta, CA 93116
800-647-9882 • 805-692-0043 • Fax 805-967-5155
www.queenship.org

Printed in the United states of America

ISBN:1-57918-297-6

Contents

Foreword

Father Matthew Buettner's new book on the Mass should be entitled, "Si scires donum Dei" (If you knew the gift of God...), for its whole purpose is to make Roman Catholics realize the incomparable gift that Christ has given them in the Holy Sacrifice of the Mass. Our Lord promised His disciples that "He would not leave them orphans" and has by these words guaranteed that He would continue to be fully present in His Holy Bride and in the Holy Sacrifice of the Mass – an unbloody repetition of His ultimate sacrifice on Calvary.

Most Catholics' ignorance of what the Mass truly is should make the angels weep, they who invisibly surround the altar silently singing Sanctus, Sanctus, Sanctus, while witnessing the indifference of thousands of the faithful who go to Mass because it is commanded, but have no inkling of what is taking place. This explains in part their lack of reverence, their chatting, their way of dressing, their "boredom."

This tragic ignorance, and therefore total lack of appreciation for the greatest of all gifts, Christ made reference to in the parable of the king who invited guests to his son's wedding feast. All of them found "plausible" excuses and turned down this royal invitation. Irate, the king ordered his servants to go out into the thoroughfares and invite all those they met so that the wedding hall would be full. His servants obeyed his order. But the king noticed that one of the guests came without having put on a wedding garment. We know the end of the story: this man was thrown into the outer darkness (Matthew 22:1-14).

Meditating upon this sad episode, we observe that the "honorable" guests – imprisoned in their mediocrity – had neither the understanding for the honor conferred upon them by the kingly invitation, nor gratitude for this great gift. Like Esau (a role model of the society in which we live) they were selling their birthright for a mess of pottage. Their hierarchy of values was so totally distorted that they were blind to their arrogant irreverence. They were replaced by "substitutes" who filled the wedding hall. One of them, however, came dressed as if he was going to a country fair. This is what is happening in many a Catholic Church every Sunday. "Come as you are" is now an acceptable custom. This applies, for example, not only to the shameless way in which some people dress – especially during the summer when parishioners dare to come to Mass and receive Holy Communion in beach attire – it also applies to the negligent posture which many adopt: there is a dignified way of sitting or of standing. There is an "I don't care" attitude which is acceptable in a gym, but not in a sacred place.

Finally, many so-called Catholics seem to have no idea that Catholic Churches are consecrated places, that is, made sacred. It is said in the Liturgy: "terribilis est locus iste: hic domus Dei est, et porta coeli..." (fearful is this place: here is the house of God, the gate of heaven). The invisible angels are trembling in awe; many Catholics enter this sacred space as if it were an entertainment hall.

Father Buettner's book aims at remedying this tragic situation. It has one great and noble purpose: to make Catholics conscious that what takes place during Mass is an event of earth-shaking dimension; it is the re-presentation of the Sacrifice of Calvary – Christ offering Himself to His Father for the redemption of our sinful humanity, which had crucified Him.

Faith, and faith alone, can cause us to see that everything else, without exception, pales by comparison with the awesomeness of what is taking place when the priest, representing Christ, pronounces the words, "Hoc est enim Corpus meum" (This is my Body). In the wake of Vatican II, very many Catholics

– alas, even priests – seem to have totally lost sight of what the Mass is. Catholic education is at its lowest possible level: children going to so-called Catholic schools are abysmally ignorant of the most elementary dogmas of the Faith; in many cases, Catholic teaching is so watered down that it is poisoned by secular ideals. Are seminaries much better? Some are faithful, but they are the minority. Tragically, after the Council, the Catholic Faith was either not taught or was distorted or so watered down that the minds of the faithful became confused, and their hearts remain cold. Father Buettner's book is, then, invaluable. For each of it twenty-six sections informs the faithful of the structure, the meaning, the sacredness of the Holy Mass. Like a symphony, it moves step by step to a climax – to the Consecration of bread and wine which actually become the Body and Blood of our Savior and King.

Originally published in a series of articles, but now in book form, each section illuminates for the reader the meaning of the part of the Mass examined and then leads organically to the next part. Like a golden chain, each one of them prepares for the next; the last one is the last link that crowns the precious gem of supernatural events. The language is limpid, clear. It can be grasped by young and old. It captivates one's attention and opens up the treasures of the magnificent Catholic Mass.

How I wish that it could be made obligatory in every single diocese. Those who have ears to hear will be fecundated by the sublime teaching of a sacrifice in which Christ is present and tells us, "He who eats my flesh and drinks my blood" will have eternal life. Indeed, the title of this book should be Si scires donum Dei.

Tolle, lege.

Dr. Alice von Hildebrand
New Rochelle, New York
21 November 2005

A portion of the proceeds of this book benefits

The Te Deum Foundation Inc.

For additional copies and further information please visit
www.tedeumfoundation.org

Introduction

"The Holy Mass is both the means and the sign through
which the Lord bequeaths us his love." [1]

Adrienne von Speyr, Swiss mystic of last century and close
spiritual confident to the acclaimed theologian, Hans Urs von
Balthasar, dictated her reflections on the spiritual significance
of the Holy Sacrifice of the Mass, the substance of which
became a short book simply entitled, "The Holy Mass." In
this work, Von Speyr continues,

[The Lord's] whole life was a Eucharist to the Father, and it
is in this, his Eucharist, that he wants to include all his people.
Christian thanksgiving is fulfilled in and cannot be separated
from the wholeness of the Holy Mass, itself a commemoration
of the wholeness of the love of the Lord. Each celebration of
the Holy Mass is a unique introduction to the love of the Lord.
No single Holy Mass is to be considered in itself, but rather
it stands in relation to all other Holy Masses, which together
form the indivisible sign of the whole and indivisible love of
the Lord for his Church. [2]

This introduction to Von Speyr's profound spiritual
reflections on the Holy Mass not only serves as a beneficial
point of departure for our present reflections on the Holy Mass,
but more precisely the proper spiritual lens or perspective
through which we must enter this study. The Holy Mass is,
indeed, the highest expression of human love and thanksgiving
offered to the Eternal Father by the Son on our behalf, as well as
the fullest expression of the divine love of the Father offered to
mankind. Without this proper perspective, our study remains a
mere academic exercise, a course in the Holy Mass, rather than

---

1   Adrienne von Speyr, *The Holy Mass* (San Francisco, CA: Ignatius Press,
     1999), 7-9.
2   *Ibid.,* 11.

a faithful investigation of what the Lord has entrusted to his beloved Bride, the Church, as a memorial of his love.

As we now approach this study of the Holy Sacrifice of the Mass, the reader would benefit by considering the following items:

1. As with any study of a spiritual and theological nature, it is recommended that one approach this material with faith, humility, and prayer.

2. The following study is not intended to be exhaustive, but rather the opposite: these lessons are meant to introduce the reader to the basic understanding of the mystery of the Mass. More profound theological and philosophical examinations are readily available (a bibliographical list of resources is included at the end). Thus, the intended audience of these lessons is the Catholic layman or interested non-Catholic, devout Mass attendee or prospective convert.

3. The origin of this material is rather unique and is worth mentioning. As a response to Pope John Paul II's "Year of the Eucharist," I decided to provide a comprehensive catechesis on the Holy Mass for my parishioners, to assist them in understanding the mystery and beauty of the Holy Mass. And so, we began in October 2004. We examined the Holy Mass one part at a time, one week at a time. Twenty-seven lessons later, we finished providentially on the Solemnity of Corpus Christi. Additionally, it was recommended that I publish these 5-minute lectures in our diocesan newspaper, "The Catholic News and Herald," to provide a greater catechetical outreach to the Diocese of Charlotte. The response was overwhelming. Catholics throughout the diocese, as well as my own parishioners, have requested that these lectures be compiled and published to make them more accessible. This present book is a response to that desire.

4. Finally, one should consider that these lectures were

originally designed to be delivered before the conclusion of the Holy Mass and only secondarily printed and read. Therefore, I have revised them and included footnotes for further consultation and study. The lessons are slightly altered from their original format to provide a more scholarly approach. My only desire in these lectures is that they will aid and assist all of us in our "Understanding the Mystery of the Mass."

Fr. Matthew Buettner,
November 2005

About the Author

A native of Peoria, Illinois, Fr. Matthew Buettner received the Bachelor of Arts in Philosophy from Saint Charles Borromeo Seminary in Philadelphia and the Master of Divinity from Catholic University in Washington, DC, before he was ordained to the Priesthood in 2003. He served as Parochial Vicar at Saint Gabriel's Catholic Church in Charlotte, NC for a year prior to transferring to Saint Dorothy's Catholic Church in Lincolnton, NC, where he has served as Parochial Vicar since July 2004.

1

Dignum et Iustum Est

In a homily given by Pope John Paul II just months before his death, the Holy Father designated the time between 17 October 2004 and 29 October 2005 as "The Year of the Eucharist."[1] During this year, we have the wonderful privilege to commemorate and devote ourselves more faithfully to Our Lord, who is truly present in the Holy Eucharist.

During this year designated to the sacrament of Our Lord's Body and Blood, we would benefit greatly by contemplating the tremendous mystery of the Holy Sacrifice of the Mass and the gift of the Holy Eucharist. In doing so, we are not about to explain away the mystery that has physically, spiritually, and intellectually nourished the Church for 2000 years. Our task is to discover, or rather rediscover the fruits of our redemption purchased by the sacrifice of Jesus Christ on our behalf and expressed most profoundly in the Holy Sacrifice of the Mass. In these reflections, we are going to spend the better part of this year devoted to the Holy Eucharist to penetrate more deeply into the mystery of the Sacrifice of the Mass and the sacrament of the altar. And so without further consideration, our discussion begins with the end. What is the purpose of the Mass? Why do we go to Mass? Let us answer the latter first.

We go to Mass because God obliges us, commands us, and even demands our presence at Mass each week. He is the benevolent King who imposes a weekly summons on his subjects to enter his holy court. Recall that for thousands of years, ever since God led the Israelites, his people, from slavery in Egypt to the freedom of the Promised Land, he has commanded his chosen people to "Keep Holy the Sabbath".[2]

---

1   Homily of Pope John Paul II Announcing the Year of the Eucharist, *Corpus Christi Sunday*, Basilica of St. John Lateran, Rome, Italy: 10 June 2004.

2   Exodus 19:8-11

1

For the Jews, this meant the strict observance of rest from labor in order to be refreshed. Man is to imitate God his Creator who rested from the 6 days of work on the 7th day. And on this Sabbath day ("Sabbath" literally means "seventh"), man is to recall the goodness of God in delivering his people from slavery, to remember God's covenant with his people, and to praise, worship, and adore God. And for Christians, we recall the fulfillment of God's saving work in Jesus Christ, who releases man from the spiritual bondage of sin and death. Man is still obliged by God to "Keep Holy the Sabbath" even though the Sabbath for Christians is not marked on Saturday, the 7th day, but Sunday, which is the first day of the new creation, the 8th day. So essential is keeping "Holy the Sabbath Day" that the first precept of the Church is to "Attend Mass on Sundays and Holy Days of obligation."[3] Failure to do so without a good mitigating reason is considered grave matter and can separate us from God.[4]

So why does God oblige us to attend Mass? Ultimately, there are two reasons. First, dignum et iustum est: "It is right to give thanks and praise."[5] The Mass teaches us the ultimate reason for attending the Mass is that God deserves it. All that we are and all that we have been given is a gratuitous gift from God. We cannot earn his love; we cannot merit his grace; we cannot purchase life without end. All is a divine gift. Therefore, we are fundamentally in debt to God. And since God creates us for himself, to honor him, to adore him, and to serve him alone, we are bound by the duty of justice to offer him the greatest sacrifice of praise that is humanly possible. Justice demands that God, who is perfect, receive a perfect sacrifice of praise. But man, estranged from God since the Original Sin of Adam and Eve, is essentially incapable of offering a perfect sacrifice; that is, until God became man and

---

3   *Catechism of the Catholic Church*, 2180.
4   *Ibid.*, 2181.
5   Roman Missal, Preface dialogue to the Eucharistic Prayer.

offered himself on our behalf. And this brings us to the second ultimate reason for attending Mass.

We not only render to God the praise he is due at Mass, but we do so principally through Jesus Christ, the High Priest.[6] At Mass, we unite ourselves with the worship of the Son unto the Father in the Holy Spirit. By recalling the events of Christ's passion, death, and resurrection, we are truly present at Calvary, present when Christ offered the one perfect sacrifice of his body and blood to the Father and then offered the fruits of his sacrifice to you and me.[7] Christ's sacrifice is the perfect expression of divine justice and divine mercy. And in recalling these same events day after day, week after week, year after year, we approach our goal, which is eternal salvation.

And so, God commands us to "Keep Holy the Sabbath" and obliges us to attend Mass in order to worship Him through the perfect worship of His own Son so that we may receive the sacramental gift of our redemption, the Body and Blood of Christ. In our next consideration, we will examine how to prepare ourselves for the Holy Sacrifice of the Mass.

---

6   *Ibid.,* 1368.

7   *Ibid.,* 1362-1367.

2
According to the
Mode of the Receiver

Previously, we recognized that God still commands his people to "Keep Holy the Sabbath." As Christians, we do so by fulfilling the first precept of the Church: attending Mass every Sunday and holy day of obligation.[8] By participating in the Holy Sacrifice of the Mass, we hope to attain the two-fold purpose or goal of the Mass: 1) to give glory to God by praising, adoring, and worshiping the Father through the Son in the Holy Spirit, and 2) receiving the fruits of Christ's passion, death, and resurrection in Holy Communion. In short, we come to Mass prepared to give and to receive: the two reciprocal parts or activities of any relationship of love. And like any relationship, our relationship with God, expressed so fully and completely through the Mass, requires time, effort, desire and dedication, indeed, preparation, in order to receive what God has prepared. Therefore it is essential to spend a few moments considering our need to prepare for the Holy Mass.

Throughout the Middle Ages, there was a very commonly used philosophical principle chiefly articulated and employed by Scholasticism.[9] The philosophical principle was thus stated: "What is received is received according to the mode of the receiver." What does this mean in everyday language?

Suppose two friends attend the Charlotte Symphony Orchestra. Both are musicians. One of them plays the drums in a rock band. The other musician plays the cello in a local string quartet. Considering that both are listening to the same

---

8   *Ibid.*, 2042.
9   Scholasticism is the synthesis of Aristotelian philosophy and Christian revelation in medieval European thought. It basically sought to resolve the conflicts of faith and reason and of nominalism and realism, and to establish proofs for the existence of God.

symphony and the same music, which of these two do you think will receive more from the performance, appreciate the beauty and the intricacies of the music?

Or suppose there are two identical windows in the same bedroom. One of them is dusty and dirty. The other window is clean and clear. Given that the sun is shining outside, which window will allow more light to pass through and brighten the room?

Both examples demonstrate the principle that "What is received is received according to the mode of the receiver." In both cases, there is an objective reality, whether it is the beautiful music of a symphony or the light of the sun. Each passes through the receiver differently, depending upon the mode or receptivity or disposition of the receiver.

Similarly, there is an objective reality, an objective truth in the Mass, that by divine power, through the instrumentation of the priest acting in persona Christi (in the person of Christ), bread and wine are changed into the Body and Blood, Soul and Divinity of Jesus Christ. This truth does not depend upon individual belief, just as the fact that the sky is blue is independent of individual belief.[10] However, the graces that we receive from this sacrament depend upon our receptivity, our disposition, our readiness to receive them. We receive grace to the extent that we are prepared to receive. Grace is not magic. Grace is not automatic. Assisting at the Holy Mass is not at all like using a vending machine: We show up, put a little money in the collection, and receive Holy Communion and grace. No. This is not the kind of giving and receiving that is characteristic of loving relationships.

Since the graces that we receive depend upon our receptivity, our disposition, our readiness, how should we prepare for Mass? First, we must be in a state of grace to receive Holy Communion.[11] That does not mean that we have

---

10   *Ibid.,* 1375-1376.
11   *Ibid.,* 1415.

to be perfect. But we must not be conscious of any mortal sins. If a person is conscious of any mortal sins, he must first go to the sacrament of Penance before he can be admitted to Holy Communion. If he receives Holy Communion conscious of mortal sins, he commits a further sin of sacrilege. And so, as St. Paul states in his first letter to the Corinthians: "Whoever eats the bread or drinks the cup of the Lord in an unworthy manner will be guilty of profaning the body and blood of the Lord".[12] On the other hand, if we receive worthily, in a state of grace, along with the Body and Blood of Christ, we also receive immense graces, numerous blessings—we receive the gift of our redemption. The light of God's grace can only penetrate into the soul insofar as the soul is purified.

Besides approaching the sacred mysteries in a state of grace, we can also prepare for the Holy Sacrifice of the Mass with prayer. Prayer establishes the ongoing communication that we need to give and receive during the Mass. The holy exchange of gifts in the Mass is accomplished through the exercise of prayer, through speaking to God and listening to him. And so, this requires us to arrive early, with adequate time to prepare our souls for the Mass.[13]

In order to arrive at our two-fold goal of giving God due worship and receiving the gift of our redemption, we must prepare our souls adequately to receive his grace, which is not magic or automatic. "What is received is received according to the mode of the receiver." We must develop our ear for the beautiful rhythm and harmony of prayer, which is often punctuated by periods of silence; we must keep the window of our soul clean to allow divine love and grace to transform us with our cooperation.

In our next consideration, we will continue our foundational material on the Mass by considering the Mass as a sacred ritual.

---

12   I Cor. 11:27
13   See Appendix B for Suggested Prayers in Preparation for the Holy Sacrifice of the Mass

3
Sacred Ritual

We began our catechesis on the Holy Sacrifice of the Mass by looking at the purpose or the goal of the Mass, which is to worship God as perfectly as possible and receive God's grace through the reception of Holy Communion. Since this is our highest goal or duty in life, the last lesson acknowledged our need to prepare for Mass. We saw that the best preparation for Mass is to live a life of virtue, overcoming sin in our lives, as well as taking time to pray before Mass begins. This time we are going to take a moment to look at how we are to arrive at our goal. If our goal is to drive from Charlotte, NC to Washington, DC, should we not take a moment to look over a road map before we depart? We will now look at the "road map," the schema of the Mass, commonly known as the "ritual."

Ritual is a natural part of human life. A good number of our daily activities are marked by ritual: from our morning rituals, to driving from place to place, to cooking a meal and going to rest at night. In fact, the philosophers have called man a "ritual-making animal." Rituals mark the day, the week, and the season. Most of us probably have a specific family ritual for the seasons and the feasts throughout the year, such as birthdays, Christmas, and Easter.

The family of God also has its rituals. But the difference is that in God's family, God, as our Father, establishes the ritual that we are to follow. God is the author and the legislator of sacred ritual. Indeed, if our goal is to worship God as perfectly as we are able, it would make sense that he would teach us how, even demonstrate the way it is to be done; it would make sense that he would provide us with an accurate road map that leads to worship that is pleasing to him. Otherwise, we might

7

be wandering aimlessly about with no sense of our path or the destination. Therefore, God has provided the Mass as a sacred ritual that we can follow to worship him perfectly.

Not only does God establish the ritual of the Holy Mass so that we can worship him in a way that is truly pleasing, arriving at our destination, but he gives us the Holy Mass because it is most suited to us as his children. When we are baptized, we become members of the Body of Christ, adopted sons and daughters of the heavenly Father. And as members of his family, we worship him as a family, as a communion of faith. Ritual allows common expression of faith that spans time and place, culture and language. It is one of the marks or characteristics of the Catholic Church that we share a universal faith and practice with all Catholics throughout the world. The Mass that we attend today is the same Mass that is being offered in St. Peter's Basilica in Rome by the Pope. When you are on vacation in Italy or England or the Philippines, you can attend the same Catholic Mass that is being offered in Lincolnton, NC. Ritual allows communal expression of faith throughout the world and throughout time.

Perhaps more importantly than allowing communal expression of faith, ritual also encourages true freedom. Some people may think that ritual binds or constricts or stifles freedom of expression. But in reality, ritual encourages freedom. The modern mind often misunderstands freedom. All too often, the modern mind confuses freedom with liberty or license. Imagine a communal worship service that did not follow a ritual. How free would the congregation be to participate? Would you know what to expect next? When it comes to driving, the rules of the road encourage the freedom of drivers to arrive safely at their destination. It is when a driver decides to be novel or innovative in his approach to the speed limit or stop lights or other such rules that accidents occur. Like the rules of driving, ritual establishes a familiar pattern. This familiar pattern of worship allows free access to the sacred mysteries. Ritual is like the two banks of a river that direct the flow of that river towards its destination. Ritual frees the mind and the heart to respond to God's grace and allows us to pray more effectively. In lesson four we will conclude our background material on the Mass by looking at how Our Lord established the sacred ritual of the Mass within the context of another sacred ritual: the Passover.

4
From the Passover
to the Paschal Mystery

Over the past three presentations, we have reiterated that the end or goal or purpose of the Holy Mass is to worship God as perfectly as we are capable. If our goal is to worship God as perfectly as possible, it would make sense that he would teach us how, even demonstrate the way it is to be done; it would make sense that he would provide us with an accurate method that pleases him. That is why last week we recognized that God is the author and the legislator of sacred ritual. As Christians, we always follow the example of Jesus Christ. Because Jesus is God, he has divine authority to establish and demonstrate the form of worship that is most pleasing to the Father; as man, he perfectly accomplishes it on our behalf and left us an example to follow. So, what did Christ establish as the perfect worship and how did he do it?

We read in Sacred Scripture that on the night before he died, Jesus Christ celebrated the Passover with his apostles.[14] During the meal, Our Lord fulfilled the meaning of the Passover and instituted the new and everlasting covenant. The Last Supper became the First Mass. Since the Passover formed the context of the First Mass, we need to look for a moment at the significance of the Passover.

In the Old Testament Book of Exodus, we discover that after the Israelites were enslaved to the Egyptians for approximately 400 years, Moses negotiated with Pharaoh for the release of the Israelite slaves from bondage.[15] Before the final plague, the death of the first-born, God told Moses to instruct the Israelites to kill the Passover lamb, to take a bunch of hyssop

---

14   Cf. *Catechism*, 1339; Matthew 26:17-29; Mark 14:12-25; Luke 22:7-20; I Cor 11:23-26.
15   Exodus 5ff

and dip it in the blood, and spread the lamb's blood over the doorposts of their houses. That evening, when the destroyer arrived to slay the first-born in the land of Egypt, he passed over the houses of the Israelites and killed the first-born of the land of Egypt. Pharaoh finally let the Israelites go—they were saved, released from political bondage, as well as spiritual bondage, since the Jews were not allowed to worship God as he commanded. Consequently, God instituted the Passover as an annual memorial to remind the Jews that God delivered them from slavery to freedom. In the Old Testament, God instructed his people how to worship him through the ritual re-presentation of the Passover.[16]

And in the New Testament, God himself would fulfill the meaning of the Passover by bringing it to its completion in the new Passover: the passion, death, and resurrection of Jesus Christ.[17] We read in Sacred Scripture that during the Passover meal,

> The Lord Jesus on the night when he was betrayed took bread, and when he had given thanks, he broke it, and said, 'This is my body which is for you. Do this in remembrance of me.' In the same way also the cup, after supper, saying, 'This cup is the new covenant in my blood. Do this, as often as you drink it, in remembrance of me'.[18]

The Passover meal is now fulfilled. In the Old Testament, the Jews sacrificed the Passover lamb. They ate the flesh of the lamb and its blood saved them from political and spiritual slavery. In the New Testament, Jesus sacrificed himself as "the Lamb of God who takes away the sins of the world."[19] He

---

16 Exodus 12
17 *Catechism, 1340.*
18 I Cor. 11:23-25
19 Cf. John 1:29

offers to us his flesh to eat and his blood delivers us from the spiritual slavery of sin. In the Old Testament, God instructed his people how to worship him through the re-presentation of the Passover. In the New Testament, the Son of God instructed his apostles to worship the Father through the re-presentation of the Holy Sacrifice of the Mass. The Mass re-presents and makes present the perfect sacrifice of Christ on Calvary, which brought glory to the Father and redemption to mankind. For 2000 years now, the Church has faithfully followed the command of the Lord to "Do this in remembrance of me." [20] Christ demonstrates the form and pattern of perfect worship, the kind of worship that is pleasing to the Father. This lesson concludes our background material on the Mass. In the following lessons, we will begin to look at this pattern of worship that God established for us to follow.

---

20   *Catechism*, 1341-1344.

5
Introibo Ad Altare Dei

We just concluded our introductory material on the Mass. We recognized that Jesus Christ fulfilled the Old Testament Passover ritual with his sacrifice, which he instituted at the Last Supper, the First Mass. This time, we begin the longer and more arduous task of examining this ritual established by Our Lord and developed by his Church. It is essential to note that the heart of the Mass, the consecration of the bread and wine into the Body and Blood, Soul and Divinity of Christ, was demonstrated by Our Lord and given to his Church. This act is manifestly attributed to Our Lord. The remainder of the Mass developed organically as the Holy Spirit has inspired the Church through the centuries. We will come to discover that every ritual, activity, posture, and response is laden with meaning from Sacred Scripture and Sacred Tradition. Therefore, the purpose of these teachings is to reveal the more profound meaning within each action of the Mass.

Before each Holy Sacrifice of the Mass begins, the celebrant and the ministers must first enter the sanctuary. This ritual is known as the entrance procession and is accompanied by the opening hymn, which prepares the faithful to unite their minds and hearts to the worship of God. This is the first of two major processions in the Mass. (Later, we will examine the second procession: when the faithful process forward to receive Holy Communion. The procession with the gifts of bread and wine could also be included as an important part of the offertory.) The entrance procession includes the celebrant, either a bishop or a priest, any concelebrating priests, deacons (if there is no deacon, a lector may carry the Book of the Gospels in the entrance procession), and the altar servers. What is the meaning of this procession?

The entrance procession represents Our Lord's earthly pilgrimage to Jerusalem. When Jesus arrived in Jerusalem, he processed through the streets on a donkey to shouts of joy and victory by the awaiting crowd who held palm branches and welcomed him in song.[21] Once a year, we recall this event liturgically on Palm Sunday.[22] Within one week, this same crowd demanded the crucifixion and death of their King.[23] And so Christ would enter the sanctuary of Calvary wearing a crown of thorns to be enthroned upon the cross. From the cross, Our Lord and King was victorious as he defeated sin, conquered death, and redeemed mankind. And so, for centuries the priest would arrive at the steps of the sanctuary and recite psalm 42 along with the altar boy: "Introibo ad altare Dei." "Ad Deum qui laetificat iuventutem meam."[24] Our Lord and King is about to enter the sanctuary in order to defeat evil, sin, and Satan once again. The entrance procession is a time for joy and victory, for our salvation is near!

Upon entering the sanctuary, the priest and ministers genuflect to the Blessed Sacrament reserved in the tabernacle (if the tabernacle is located in the sanctuary or otherwise they make a profound bow to the altar).[25] The celebrant, concelebrating priests, and deacons then reverence the altar with a kiss. The altar, which takes central importance in the sanctuary, has always been considered the greatest sign for Christ, whose own body became the altar upon which he would sacrifice himself to the Father. It is the focal point of the Holy Mass and the juncture between heaven and earth, time and eternity. The altar is consecrated with Sacred Chrism

21 Matthew 21:1-10; Mark 11:1-10; Luke 19:29-38; John 12:12-19
22 Palm Sunday marks the beginning of Holy Week; one week prior to Easter Sunday.
23 Matthew 27:22
24 "I will go unto the Altar of God." "To God, who gives joy to my youth."
25 *General Instruction of the Roman Missal* (GIRM), 274; 49.

and usually contains a relic of a saint.[26] The relics in the altar have a two-fold significance: 1) Many altars were erected over the tombs of Christians in the catacombs in the early life of the Church and 2) the Mass unites the sacrifice of a martyr's life with the sacrifice of Christ in the Holy Mass. Due to its precedence, the altar may receive the first incensation (three others may follow throughout the Mass).[27] The sweet aroma of incense prepares the altar for sacrifice and may be used in any Mass. Of all the symbolic ceremonies in the Mass, the use of incense is perhaps the oldest and the most wide-spread ritual, historically found in Jewish, Greek, and Roman ceremonies. It is also mentioned extensively in Sacred Scripture, especially in reference to the worship of God.

Now that the celebrant has ascended the steps of the sanctuary of Jerusalem, reverenced the altar with a kiss and incensed it, the Mass is ready to begin.

---

26   GIRM, 296; 302.
27   GIRM, 49; 276.

6

DOMINUS VOBISCUM

The ritual of the Mass is divided into two distinct parts: the Liturgy of the Word and the Liturgy of the Eucharist. Each of these is subdivided into smaller parts called rituals or the abbreviated version, "rites." Since the Holy Sacrifice of the Mass has a structure and character that is universal and formal, the celebrant need only to follow the directions of the ritual: to read the prayers and perform the actions set out in the Roman Missal.[28] As we mentioned above, following the sacred ritual allows the freedom of both the celebrant and the congregation to participate in the Mass. And so the Holy Mass begins with a short ritual known as the "Introductory Rites," which include the Sign of the Cross, the formal greeting, the "Penitential Rite," the Gloria, and the Opening Collect or Prayer. The purpose of these "Introductory Rites" is to draw us into prayer and to prepare our hearts and minds to listen to God's Word and to participate in his sacrifice.[29] In our last teaching, we followed the celebrant as he processed into the sanctuary, reverenced the altar with a kiss and incensed it. The celebrant arrives at the chair. And so the Holy Mass begins.

Notice that the Holy Sacrifice of the Mass does not begin with an informal greeting by a lector or cantor, welcoming people to the parish. The Mass does not begin with "Good morning" or "Did you catch the game last night?" or "Nice weather we're having!" or other commentary by the celebrant. Rather, the Holy Mass begins "In the name of the Father, and of the Son, and of the Holy Spirit." We begin the Mass as we begin all prayer: by addressing God, greeting the Blessed Trinity, through whom and by whom the Mass is celebrated. The Sign of the Cross marks the beginning of the Mass, as

---

28   Cf. *Redemptionis Sacramentum*, 11.
29   Cf. GIRM, 46.

well as the end of the Mass with the final blessing. Although the ritual of the Mass is divided into parts, it is "one single act of worship".[30] And so, from beginning to end the Holy Sacrifice of the Mass is accomplished "in the name" of God; it is the opus Dei, the work of God, which we enter as we begin the Mass.

Beginning with the Sign of the Cross reminds us that we gain access to the Father by virtue of our baptism: we were introduced to the cross as it was signed upon our foreheads and holy water was poured over our head three times in the name of each person of the Blessed Trinity. Baptism consecrates us as adopted sons and daughters of the heavenly Father who can now enter into the saving mysteries of the Son accomplished on our behalf. The Sign of the Cross is used throughout the Mass to bless and consecrate, for it is by the power of the cross of Christ that our redemption was won and our sanctification is completed.

Following the Sign of the Cross, the celebrant greets the congregation, not in his own words, but with words taken from Sacred Scripture, found in the epistles of St. Paul. There are three options for the priest, either "The grace of Our Lord Jesus Christ and the love of God and the fellowship of the Holy Spirit be with you all" or "The grace and peace of God the Father and the Lord Jesus Christ be with you" or simply, "The Lord be with you" ["Dominus Vobiscum"].[31] Only the bishop says, "Peace be with you" ["Pax Vobiscum"] by virtue of his office as vicar of Christ, recalling the inaugural words of Our Lord to his apostles after his resurrection.[32]

The congregation responds, "And also with you." ["Et cum spiritu tuo," which is more precisely translated as, "And

---

30 *Sacrosanctum Concilium,* 56.
31 Many of the texts of the official Latin edition, the **Edicion Typica,** are given to show the official Latin form of the Mass texts, as well as the current approved English translations, which may be rendered more closely to the official texts in the near future.
32 John 20:19-23

with your spirit."] This exchange between the celebrant and the congregation completes the first dialogue of the Mass, expressing the reciprocal conversation between Christ, the head, and the Church, his Mystical Body. In our next consideration, we will complete our discussion of the "Introductory Rites" by examining the "Penitential Rite."

7
Kyrie Eleison

W e have already begun our discussion of the Introductory Rites of the Holy Sacrifice of the Mass. We discussed the entrance procession, incensation of the altar, the Sign of the Cross, and the celebrant's formal greeting. We continue our discussion of the Introductory Rites by examining the "Penitential Rite." And as we enter this discussion of the Penitential Rite, we discover that we are in the midst of a conversation on prayer.

As we mentioned earlier, from beginning to end the Mass is a prayer—in fact, the highest act of prayer known to mankind, since the Mass is the worship of the Son of God unto the Father. As members of Christ's Mystical Body, the Church, we participate in his perfect worship. The Mass therefore teaches us how to pray, educates us in the language and grammar of prayer. And the first lesson of prayer, the primary movement of the Mass, is one of humility. In imitation of Christ, the Son of God who humbled himself to become man, who humbled himself to take upon himself our sins, who humbled himself to undergo his passion, crucifixion, and death on our behalf, we must humble ourselves. And so the Church seeks to imitate the humility of Christ by first recognizing our sins and acknowledging the fact that we are sinners in desperate need of God's abundant mercy. We must first recognize that we are empty, before we can be filled. Therefore, the celebrant invites us to pause, examine our conscience in silence, and ask for God's mercy and forgiveness.

During this brief moment of silence at the beginning of the Holy Mass, we might be wondering what to think about: What I did last night or the child that is disrupting my peace or what to eat for breakfast after Mass? During these precious moments, we should examine our conscience, recalling individual sins. Above all, we need to become aware of our overall need for forgiveness and mercy for the sins that we have committed and the good we have omitted, which we may have forgotten. It is a moment to prepare our souls to abandon our old sinful habits and seek the grace and mercy that God has prepared for us in receiving his Body and Blood in Holy Communion. If we become conscious of having committed mortal sins, we should resolve to go to the Sacrament of Penance as soon as possible and refrain from receiving Holy Communion. Although the Penitential Rite does not grant absolution for mortal sins, it does help us to receive forgiveness for our less serious sins, venial sins, which are forgiven when we receive Holy Communion with humility and love.[33]

After a few moments of silence, the celebrant may begin a prayer, known by its first word in Latin, the Confiteor: "I confess to Almighty God…." Otherwise, he may lead one of two other optional prayers that request, "Lord, have mercy." When we pray the Confiteor as a community, we confess that we are guilty of sins in thought, word, and deed. Then, we seek the intercession of: "Blessed Mary, ever Virgin," who was conceived without sin and remained sinless throughout her life, the angels, who battle with Satan and defeat evil, the saints, who were sinners like us, but cooperated with God's grace and mercy to defeat their own sinfulness and persevered in holiness of life, and finally, the members of the Church Militant (the pilgrim Church on earth), "and you, my brothers and sisters, to pray to the Lord our God for me." The celebrant completes this prayer with a prayer that begs for God's mercy, seeks forgiveness, and leads us to heaven.

Finally, the Penitential Rite may close with the ancient threefold litany: Kyrie eleison, Christe eleison, Kyrie eleison ("Lord have mercy, Christ have mercy, Lord have mercy").

---

33   GIRM, 51.

This litany of mercy is the only surviving vestige of the Greek language remaining in the Latin Rite of the Catholic Church. Whether the Mass is offered in Latin, English, Spanish, or German, this Greek prayer may be recited by the celebrant or deacon or may be chanted by the celebrant, deacon, or cantor. This formula, "Lord, have mercy" really comes straight from the Gospel. Oftentimes a great healing by Christ is preceded by the humble cry of a beggar, "Son of David, have mercy on me!"[34]   That is precisely where we find ourselves at the beginning of Mass: poor beggars in need of God's mercy. And that is why we approach the throne of our Heavenly Father in humility from the very beginning.   Now that we have acknowledged our sinfulness before God and our neighbor, we now sing the Biblical hymn of praise, known by its first word in Latin, The Gloria.

---

34   Cf. Mark 10:46-52; Matthew 15:21ff; Luke 17:13

8
Gloria in excelsis Deo

We mentioned last time that the Mass is the greatest prayer of the Church. As the highest act of prayer, the Mass teaches us how to pray. The first movement of the heart in prayer is humility and so we enter into the Mass by first calling to mind our sins and seeking the Divine Mercy of God in the Penitential Rite. Only then, only after recognizing our need for forgiveness and only after acknowledging the abundant mercy that God supplies in our need, are we able to sing for joy in the ancient hymn of the Gloria. And so, the Mass teaches us that prayer begins with humility and moves to praise and adoration of God: after the Penitential Rite follows the Gloria.

Upon close inspection, we will discover that there is not a single word in the Gloria which is not also found in Sacred Scripture, in the letters of St. Paul or in the writings of St. John. The Gloria is one of the oldest Christian hymns. The earliest records of the first Christians, dating as far back as the early 2nd century, refer to singing the angelic hymn, known as the Gloria in excelsis Deo ("Glory to God in the highest") before the Sacrifice of the Mass.[35] From the very beginning, singing the Gloria was particularly appropriate during the Christmas season, since the opening words of the hymn were sung by the angels after the birth of Our Lord. Later evidence shows that the Gloria was given wider range to be sung at Sunday Masses throughout the year, but only when the bishop offered the Sacrifice. It wasn't until almost the 12th century that the Gloria was extended to every Sunday Mass offered by priests, as well as bishops.[36]

---

35   Charles Belmonte, *Understanding the Mass* (Princeton, NJ: Scepter Publishers, 1989), 61; Adrian Fortesque, *The Mass: A Study of the Roman Liturgy* (Fitzwilliam, NH: Loreto Publications, 2003), 241.
36   *The Mass*, 242-243.

The Gloria is composed of three main parts and refers to the three divine persons of the Blessed Trinity. The first section praises the Father, beginning with the words of the angels to the shepherds after the birth of Our Lord: Glory to God in the highest and peace to His people on earth. The hymn continues to praise the Father: Lord God, heavenly King, almighty God and Father; We worship you, we give you thanks, we praise you for your glory. In other parts of the Mass, we thank and praise God for what he has accomplished. But here in the Gloria, we thank God for who he is, not for what he does. The second section of the Gloria is addressed to the eternal Son of God: Lord, Jesus Christ, only Son of the Father, Lord God, Lamb of God, you take away the sins of the world: have mercy on us; you are seated at the right hand of the Father: receive our prayer. Again, we praise the Son of God firstly for who he is, then for what he has accomplished. Only after recognizing the divine identity of the Son can we petition him to "receive our prayer." The hymn surges to its height and then to its completion as we move to the third section that includes reference to the Holy Spirit: For you alone are the Holy One, you alone are the Lord, you alone are the Most High, Jesus Christ, with the Holy Spirit, in the glory of God the Father. Amen. Thus completes the hymn of praise and adoration of the Blessed Trinity. It is important to note that we do not sing the Gloria during the two penitential seasons of the Church year—Advent and Lent—as a communal preparation for Christmas and Easter.

Following the Gloria, the Introductory Rites of the Mass reach their summit in the Opening Collect or Prayer. After we have approached God the Father in humility to seek his mercy and praised him for his glory, we now approach him in petition or supplication. The celebrant, speaking on behalf of the Church, collects the intentions of the day's sacrifice. He begins, "Let us pray," inviting the Church to join him in petitioning the Lord. There is a brief moment of silence to allow us the opportunity to collect our petitions and intentions. The celebrant extends his hands in prayer, known as the orans position, the typical prayer posture for the early Christians or for those who are in petition or supplication. The prayer may express an attribute or characteristic of the saint who is honored on a particular feast day, express the tone of a particular liturgical season, or simply draw together and bind various petitions to the Holy Sacrifice of the Mass. The faithful participate in this prayer by responding "Amen," which means "So be it." It is an assent to all that has been accomplished in the Introductory Rites of the Mass: from humility, to praise, and finally, to petition, which we ask through the mediation of Our Lord Jesus Christ in union with the Holy Spirit. Next, we will begin to examine the Liturgy of the Word.

9
Spiritual Foundation
for the Liturgy of the Word

We have been considering the Introductory Rites of the Mass. We discovered that as the highest form of prayer, the Mass teaches us how to pray. The Holy Sacrifice of the Mass begins with the Penitential Rite, which allows us the opportunity to confess our need for God's abundant mercy. Likewise, prayer begins with the humble recognition of one's inadequacy in the presence of God. After recognizing our sinfulness and God's abundant mercy, we are moved to praise and adore the Blessed Trinity in the ancient hymn, known as the Gloria. Likewise, prayer moves from humility and repentance to praise and adoration. Finally, the Introductory Rites of the Mass reach their culmination and fulfillment in the Opening Collect or Prayer. The celebrant collects the petitions and intercessions of the sacrifice and implores the Father through the Son in the Holy Spirit. Prayer, as in the Holy Mass, then moves from praise and adoration to petition and intercession. So far, the Introductory Rites teach us that prayer has the following form: humility and repentance, praise and adoration, petition and intercession. But there is still a further component to prayer beyond the scope of what we have already accomplished. We must listen to the voice of the Lord. We must be receptive to the Word of God. Prayer, too, becomes more receptive and meditative as we listen to the voice of God. And so the Mass moves from the Introductory Rites to the Liturgy of the Word. The congregation is seated to listen attentively as God instructs his people. Perhaps the most theologically relevant teaching on the Holy Sacrifice of the Mass, Mediator Dei, written by Pope Pius XII in 1947, explains the encounter with Christ in the Liturgy of the Word:

In the Sacred Liturgy, the whole Christ is proposed to us in all the circumstances of His life, as the Word of the Eternal Father, as born of the Virgin Mother of God, as He who teaches us truth, heals the sick, consoles the afflicted, who endures suffering and who dies; finally, as He who rose triumphantly from the dead, and who, reigning in the glory of Heaven, sends us the Holy Paraclete, and who abides in His Church forever.... The liturgy shows us Christ not only as a model to be imitated but as a Master to whom we should listen readily, a Shepherd whom we should follow, as Author of our salvation, the Source of our holiness, and the Head of the Mystical Body whose members we are, living by His very life.... Hence, the liturgical year, devotedly fostered and accompanied by the Church, is not a cold and lifeless representation of the events of the past, or a simple and bare record of a former age. It is rather Christ Himself, who is ever living in His Church.[37]

In other words, Pope Pius XII teaches that the Liturgy of the Word is not a simple recounting of historical events; it is not merely the formal reading of sacred texts; it is not a quaint reminder of our past; but rather the recapitulation of the saving work of Our Lord. Through the faithful proclamation of salvation history found in Sacred Scripture, we gain access to the saving mysteries of our faith. The events of the past are brought into the present. The mysteries of the life of Our Lord are brought into light today to continue and to fulfill the work of salvation in each generation. Christ continues his redemptive activity, his mission of teaching the truth that sets us free. As his present day disciples, we have a privileged place of honor sitting at the feet of the Master, listening to

---

37   *Mediator Dei*, 151-153; 163-165.

him, listening to the voice of the Good Shepherd leading us to eternal life. "To whom shall we go; you have the words of eternal life."[38] As St. John Eudes wrote, "We must continue to accomplish in ourselves the stages of Jesus' life and his mysteries and often to beg him to perfect and realize them in us and in his whole Church...."[39] Next time we will examine how the divine mysteries are unfolded as we look at the structure of the Liturgy of the Word.

---

38 John 6:68
39 *Liturgy of the Hours*, Friday, week 33

10
Structure of the Liturgy of the Word

We have demonstrated that the Holy Sacrifice of the Mass teaches how to pray. According to the structure of the Mass, prayer has the following form: humility and repentance, praise and adoration, and petition and intercession. These aspects of prayer particularly involve our work, that is, we speak to God. But perhaps more important than our words, our need to address our Heavenly Father, is his desire to speak to us, to reveal his will, his divine plan, indeed himself. And so both in prayer and in the Holy Sacrifice of the Mass, which is the highest form of prayer, we must listen to the voice of the Lord. We are seated to listen attentively to the voice of the Good Shepherd guiding us into eternal life; we must be receptive to Our Lord, who is called "Rabbi," the Great Teacher, who said, "I am the Way, the Truth, and the Life," for he is the eternal Word of the eternal Father.

Several lessons ago, we discussed the Holy Mass as a sacred ritual, whose parts and prayers are selected, inspired, and faithfully handed down through the centuries. In other words, the selected readings at the Mass are part of this divine plan of revelation, so that through the liturgical seasons of the Church year, the mysteries of Christ's birth, his life, his teaching and miracles, and finally his passion, death, and resurrection are unfolded each year. From week to week, the life of Our Lord is unfolded, revealed again and again, so that we can penetrate these mysteries and receive the fruits and graces of these mysteries.

Since these readings are pre-selected and handed down to us, they are not subject to the whim of the celebrant. The readings maintain the universal character of the Church — it does not matter which Roman Catholic Church you attend:

the country, the language, the local customs, etc., the same readings are provided everywhere in the world. The celebrant does not have the authority or the freedom to select his favorite readings or discard his least favorite. The Catholic faithful have the privilege and right to hear the voice of God speak to us in every reading.

Consequently, the Church offers us a three-year cycle of readings for Sunday Masses and a two-year cycle for weekday Masses. As you attend Mass each week, almost the entire canon of Sacred Scripture, almost the whole of the Bible, is proclaimed every three years. And if you attend Mass everyday, you will hear almost the entire canon of Sacred Scripture every two years. The Sunday readings follow a very simple three-year cycle: year "A" concentrates on the Gospel of St. Matthew, year "B" focuses on the Gospel of St. Mark, and year "C," the Gospel of St. Luke. These three Gospels are very similar in structure and content and are known as the Synoptic Gospels. Since the Gospel of St. John contains material that is not found in these three Gospels, St. John's Gospel is proclaimed during specific times and seasons of the year and at specific feasts, such as Christmas and Easter.

On Sundays and other solemn feast days, three readings are provided. The first reading often comes from the Old Testament and is selected to show the Old Testament foundation for the Gospel. The Old Testament foreshadows the New Testament. The New Testament completes the Old Testament. In the words of Archbishop Fulton Sheen elucidating the immemorial words of St. Augustine: "The New is in the Old concealed, the Old is in the New revealed; the New is in the Old contained, the Old is in the New explained."[40] Therefore, on Sunday, the first reading establishes a hope that is fulfilled in the Gospel. The first reading and the Gospel fit together. The Responsorial Psalm is a response to the lesson of the

---

40   Archbishop Fulton Sheen, *Life is Worth Living*, Catechetical cassette series, "Sacred Scripture"

Old Testament reading. One psalm is selected out of the 150 psalms of the Old Testament. The second reading comes from one of the New Testament Epistles, or letters, of one of the Apostles. Throughout the year, we hear the inspired accounts of St. Paul, St. Peter, St. James, or a few others. The second lesson often does not follow the pattern established by the first reading and the Gospel, but they offer specific instruction on living the Christian life. The next consideration will take an even closer examination of the Liturgy of the Word.

11
Deo Gratias

We mentioned last week that the Liturgy of the Word offers us the opportunity to listen to the voice of the Good Shepherd, who still guides his Church from his throne in heaven. At each Mass, the eternal Word of the eternal Father unfolds the mystery of our redemption from the Old Testament to the New Testament into the present day. He constantly reveals the divine plan of our salvation. And in the last lesson we continued our examination of the Liturgy of the Word by following this revelation from our first reading from the Old Testament, the Responsorial Psalm, New Testament Epistle, and finally the Holy Gospel. Let us continue our discussion by inspecting the homily or sermon which follows the reading of the Gospel.

At the conclusion of each reading from Sacred Scripture, there is a ritual indicating that the reading has ended. The Lector proclaims, "The word of the Lord" ("Verbum Domini") and we respond, "Thanks be to God" (Deo Gratias"). It is truly fitting that this ritual follow the retelling and the recounting of the events of Salvation History found in Scripture. Indeed, our souls and our minds ought to respond with great joy to the proclamation of Sacred Scripture in gratitude and thanksgiving for what God has accomplished principally through his beloved Son. The whole of Sacred Scripture is Good News to us who are in need of God's abundant mercy and love. The Liturgy of the Word reaches its summit in the proclamation of the Holy Gospel, marked by the use of incense (now the second incensation of the Mass), the joyful Alleluia chant (which in itself is a shout of praise at the Resurrection and victory of the Lord), and all stand at attention, for the words and deeds of Our Lord are about to be spoken in one of the four inspired

Gospels. Following this reading, another ritual response is exchanged, "The Gospel of the Lord" ("Verbum Domini"), "Praise to you, Lord Jesus Christ" ("Laus tibi Christe"). The faithful are then seated once again.

Until now, the Mass has maintained a strict ritual, including the ritual responses at the conclusion of each reading. But here, the celebrant departs somewhat from a formal structure in order to explain and instruct and inspire. In other words, following the Holy Gospel, the homily or sermon is the first unstructured response of man to God's saving activity in Salvation History. And so, the homily extends our response to the readings; the homily is an extended Deo Gratias for what God has accomplished and continues to accomplish in bringing about our salvation. It is important to note that only those in Holy Orders, deacons, priests, and bishops, may proclaim the Holy Gospel and preach during the Holy Sacrifice of the Mass.[41] Why? Not only do these men receive many years of theological training, but they are officially consecrated by Holy Mother Church to preach in the name of Christ: they are not to give their personal opinions and views, but rather they are deputed by the Church to speak on her behalf as an instrument of Christ.[42]

As we just mentioned, the celebrant may give either a homily or a sermon. There is a subtle distinction between the two: a homily generally focuses on the readings from Sacred Scripture, whereas a sermon usually focuses on a particular topic or theme, such as a sermon on the "Seven Deadly Sins" or a sermon on "Charity." It is also important to note the distinction between preaching and teaching. The object of preaching is to increase faith, whereas the object of teaching

---

41   GIRM, 66; *Redemptionis Sacramentum,* 64-66.

42   *RS*, 67: "It is clear that all interpretations of Sacred Scripture are to be referred back to Christ himself as the one upon whom the entire economy of salvation hinges, though this should be done in light of the specific context of the liturgical celebration."

is to increase knowledge. The ultimate purpose of the homily or sermon is to increase faith, although elements of catechesis should be included to accomplish that goal. Unfortunately, one of the difficulties about preaching in our modern day is an unreasonable expectation of the homily. We may expect the homily to provide us with our weekly dose of Catholic faith and life: history, theology, philosophy, spirituality, liturgy, morality, Scripture analysis, etc. We want it to entertain us and be completed in five minutes or less! I will never forget one Dominican motto: "One homily cannot cover everything." Deo Gratias! Thanks be to God! The following lesson will conclude our discussion of the Liturgy of the Word as we take a look at the Profession of Faith and General Intercessions.

12
Credo

In the Liturgy of the Word, Christ the Great Teacher and Good Shepherd instructs us through the faithful proclamation of Scripture. The events of Salvation History are unfolded from the Old Testament promise of a Messiah to the New Testament fulfillment in Jesus Christ, the Son of God. Following the particular lessons from Sacred Scripture is the homily or sermon, wherein the preacher inspires, encourages, and admonishes the faithful to apply the truths of Scripture to their lives in seeking the Kingdom of God. The homily or sermon is, in fact, a response to the lessons of Scripture presented in the Liturgy of the Word with the purpose of increasing faith. As a further extension of our response to the Word of God, the Profession of Faith and the General Intercessions complete the Liturgy of the Word and are the focus of this catechesis on the Mass.

The Profession of Faith is otherwise known as the Creed (from the first word in Latin, "Credo", that is "I believe"). The Creed is an ancient summary of Christian beliefs. It is a compendium of the truths of Sacred Scripture. It is historical fact that the Profession of Faith was not originally formulated for use in the Holy Sacrifice of the Mass. Rather, the Profession of Faith was framed in the early Church for a two-fold purpose: 1) As a list of affirmations recited by the believer before his or her baptism, and 2) as an antidote to the confusion and doubt caused by heresy (false teachings) about Christ and the articles of faith. [43] The Apostles' Creed was one of the earliest and most concise set of beliefs. However, due to rampant heresy and theological confusion, the elements of each symbol of faith were elaborated and given further explanation. Thus, the

---

43   Fortesque, 285-286; Belmonte, 99.

Church used the Apostles' Creed as a basis for the list of truths at the Council of Nicaea in 325, added to it at the Council of Constantinople in 381, with the final composition at the Council of Chalcedon in 451. It was this more explicit symbol of faith that first entered the Mass at the Council of Toledo in Spain in 589: "Let the Creed resound, so that the true faith may be declared in song, and that the souls of believers, in accepting that faith, may be ready to partake, in Communion, of the Body and Blood of Christ."[44] From Spain, the entrance of the Creed in the Mass spread to Western Europe, where it was eventually placed after the Holy Gospel.

Like the Gloria, the Profession of Faith can be distinguished into three parts: 1) A confession of faith in God the Father, as creator of heaven and earth; 2) A confession of faith in one Lord, Jesus Christ, the only Son of God; and 3) A confession of faith in the means of salvation, supplied by the Holy Spirit through the Church. These three parts of the Creed unite to form a body of truths that establish the foundation of orthodox (true) Christian faith and ultimately, give witness to the marvelous history of God's redemptive love.

And as a further response to the events of salvation in Scripture and in recognition of the ongoing work of salvation in the world, the faithful speak on behalf of the Church in interceding for the needs of the Church and the world. It is important to note that the General Intercessions are by definition "general," that is, they refer to the broad needs of the universal Church and the world. By definition, they are also "intercessions" or petitions, rather than prayers of thanksgiving or praise. The Church orders the sequence of intercessions: For the needs of the Church, for public authorities and the salvation of the world, for those oppressed by any need, and for the local community, including the faithful departed.[45] The General Intercessions bring closure to the Liturgy of the Word

---

44   Belmonte, 100.
45   GIRM, 70.

and bring to completion our verbal response to the Word of God. But the Holy Mass is not ended. The Word must again become "flesh and dwell among us." The one, true sacrifice of Jesus Christ, the High Priest, must again be presented. Therefore, the next lesson will begin the second part of the Mass: the Liturgy of the Eucharist.

13
The Synagogue and the Temple

We just completed the first of the two main parts of the Mass: the Liturgy of the Word. Before moving to the second part of the Mass, we would do well to review for a moment what we have learned in our examination of the Holy Sacrifice of the Mass.

The first principal point that we discovered is that the Mass is the highest and greatest form of prayer precisely because it is the perfect worship of God the Father by the Son; the Mass is the sacrificial self-offering of Jesus Christ, the High Priest, to the Father on our behalf. As members of Christ's Mystical Body, we participate in his perfect worship of the Father. His prayer becomes our prayer. Therefore, the Holy Mass teaches us how to pray, educates us in the language and grammar of prayer, and provides for us the basic elements of prayer.

As we inspected the Introductory Rites of the Mass, we proceeded through the Penitential Rite, the Kyrie Eleison, the Gloria, and finally, the Opening Collect or Prayer. We learned that prayer has the following pattern: humility and repentance, praise and adoration, and petition and intercession. The Introductory Rites move us through these elements of prayer. But there is also a further and perhaps more significant element of prayer: receptivity, listening to the voice of God. Therefore, the Mass proceeds directly to the Liturgy of the Word, where we have the opportunity to listen to the voice of the Good Shepherd leading us to eternal truth and life. We saw that the Liturgy of the Word incorporates the Old Testament and the New Testament, combines the foundation of Judaism with the fulfillment of Christianity.

We also learned that the Liturgy of the Word impels us to respond. The homily or sermon given by the bishop, priest, or deacon is the first informal response to the Word of God with the purpose of increasing faith. Then, all the faithful respond by professing the faith of the Church, which then leads us to pray on behalf of the Church for the salvation of the world in the General Intercessions. These prayers conclude the Liturgy of the Word.

But before moving on to the Liturgy of the Eucharist, it is very important to note the historical and liturgical foundation for the Mass. The Mass is not merely a Christian invention or innovation. The New Testament rests upon the Old Testament. The family tree of Christianity has Judaism at its roots. The Liturgy of the Word is the Christian fulfillment of the Jewish Synagogue. In the Synagogue, the Jews listen attentively to the proclamation of Sacred Scripture, principally the Torah, or the Law, and the Prophets. The rabbi would then interpret and explain the Scriptures. The first Christians, in fact, would attend both the Synagogue, as well as the Holy Mass, until it became clearer that Christianity fulfilled Judaism and became the New Way.

As the Liturgy of the Word is the fulfillment of the Jewish Synagogue, so also the Liturgy of the Eucharist is the fulfillment of the Jewish Temple. In the Temple in Jerusalem, live animal sacrifices were offered to God on behalf of mankind. Blood was shed as a gift, an offering, a sacrifice that symbolically represented the sacrifice of man. Life was offered for life, blood for blood, the external sacrifice of an animal representing the internal sacrifice of man. As we discover in the Old Testament, these animal sacrifices were unable to take away sin and offer life to man. And so God sent his own Son into the world. As God, he offered the one, true, eternal sacrifice of his life to the Father; as man, he offered his life on our behalf. Life was offered for life, blood for blood, but this time, Christ's sacrifice was efficacious in redeeming the world from evil, sin, and death. And so we see that the Holy

Sacrifice of the Mass unites the Jewish Synagogue with the Jewish Temple, the Word of God with the work of salvation, the Liturgy of the Word with the Liturgy of the Eucharist. The following presentation will begin to look at the Liturgy of the Eucharist as we examine the three principal movements: offering, consecration, and communion.

14
Offertory, Consecration, and Communion

As we begin to examine the Liturgy of the Eucharist, we are reminded that the drama of our redemption is accomplished by Christ in three distinct acts: his passion, death, and resurrection; Holy Thursday, Good Friday, Easter Sunday; The Last Supper, the crucifixion and death on the cross, and the empty tomb on Easter Sunday. These three acts of our redemption compose what we call the Paschal Mystery. It is the Holy Sacrifice of the Mass that invites us into the Paschal Mystery and unites us with the means of our salvation.

Within these three acts, the passion, death, and resurrection, there are three movements in the Mass that perpetuate the effects of our redemption and apply them to our individual souls. These three movements, namely, the offertory, the consecration, and the reception of Holy Communion, compose the three principal movements of the Liturgy of the Eucharist.[46] Together, these three movements unite us with the mystery of the cross, continue to bring about our salvation by applying the fruits of our redemption today, and ultimately, express the divine love and mercy of God for His people. Let us inspect for a moment these three principal movements.

The offertory. In order to apply the merits of redemption to our souls, each of us must renew the death to sin which was brought about by Christ on the cross. Christ died once and for all on the cross 2000 years ago. In imitation of his perfect sacrifice and in union with his self-offering to the Father, we offer ourselves in union with Christ. In the early Church, this was accomplished by offering the same elements that Christ

---

46   N.B. The offertory is often called "The preparation of the altar or gifts" and the Consecration is often called "The Eucharistic Prayer"

himself offered at the Last Supper, namely bread and wine. Some of each was used by the priest to offer the sacrifice. Today, we substitute money for these elements. The donated money purchases the bread and wine sacrificed at the Mass; but the money also represents ourselves, since we receive money as recompense for our labor, our time, and our talent. The material sacrifice that we make is still a symbol of our spiritual incorporation into the death of Christ. Through the free offering of ourselves to God in union with Christ we find salvation.

The Consecration. The offertory leads us to the consecration. The consecration of the Mass does not mean that Our Lord dies again, for he can never die again in his own individual human nature. But he prolongs his death in us. In the offertory we present ourselves for sacrifice with Christ; in the consecration we die and rise with him. We apply his death to ourselves that we may share his resurrection and his glory. At the consecration, the eternal sacrifice of Christ punctures the time barrier, heaven dawns upon earth, and Immanuel comes again to meet man. By the words of Christ speaking through a priest, the Holy Spirit changes the substance of bread and wine into the substance of Christ's Body and Blood, Soul and Divinity. This is known as transubstantiation (from the Latin, meaning "change in substance").[47] This is not simply a recited prayer, but a divine act which enables us to apply the merits of the cross to ourselves; the once and for all sacrifice of Christ is brought into the present and relived in us. Why? The sacrifice is re-presented by divine command in order to receive him as spiritual nourishment and as an antidote for sin and death.

Holy Communion. In the offertory, we are like lambs led to the slaughter. In the consecration, we are the lambs who are slaughtered in our old sinful selves. And in Holy Communion, we find that we have not died, but that we have

---

47   Cf. *Catechism,* 1376.

come to life. In a certain sense, the substance of bread and wine must be sacrificed, must die, so that it may become the Body and Blood of Christ. In the same way, our old habits of sin must also be sacrificed so that we might have new life in Christ. Chemicals must die that plants might live. Plants must perish that animals might live. Chemicals, plants, and animals must die, must be sacrificed, that man might live. And our old sinful selves must perish for God to live in us. That is why we "receive" Holy Communion: we receive Christ, we receive divine life. But perhaps more importantly, it is Christ who receives us, incorporating us into his divine life. In the next consideration, we will begin to inspect the rituals that bring us to union with Christ.

15
The First Movement: The Offertory

Last time, we were reminded that the Paschal Mystery, the passion, death and resurrection of Jesus Christ, is unfolded for us in every Holy Mass in three distinct movements: the offertory, the consecration, and the reception of Holy Communion. Again, we discovered that these three movements together give glory to God and bring about the fulfillment of our redemption by applying the fruits of Christ's gift of redemption to our individual souls. In this lesson, we will take a closer examination of the offertory by answering the question: What is being offered at the Holy Sacrifice of the Mass?

The Collection. The first liturgical movement of the offertory involves the collection. To support the financial needs of the clergy and the material needs of the Church is one of the six precepts of the Church.[48] But more than an obligation, we have the opportunity to participate in the missionary efforts of the Church by the funds that are collected at each Mass. Our hard-earned money pays the bills to keep the Church open and operational, supports the clergy, contributes to the work of evangelization and charity, and most notably, purchases the bread and wine that is necessary for the Mass. Obviously, we do not have the capacity to give to God the thanksgiving that He deserves for all the generous gifts we have received, but we do make the best attempt by making a sacrifice of our own resources. The money represents our own time and talent given at work. And so the collection symbolizes the more important gift of ourselves given to God.

Bread and wine. Along with the collection, bread and wine is offered by the faithful in the offertory procession at

---

48   *Catechism,* 2043.

the Mass. These elements are so necessary for the celebration of the Mass that without bread and wine, a priest is unable to offer the sacrifice of the Mass.[49] We will explore the use and significance of bread and wine in more detail in our next discussion.

Prayer, sacrifice, intentions. The collection, bread, and wine are offered and presented to the celebrant during the offertory. But more importantly, we also bring our spiritual gifts. During the offertory, we are invited to collect and present our prayers, sacrifices, and intentions that are unique to the celebration of each Mass. We are given the opportunity to unite our own prayers, the many small sacrifices that we offered throughout the day or the week, and the many intentions we bring with the perfect sacrifice of Christ in the consecration.

Ourselves. These prayers, sacrifices, and intentions are the spiritual form of the offering. When combined with the material offering of money, bread, and wine, they collectively represent the meager gift of ourselves, generously presented to God for sacrifice.

The priest. All of these are collected and presented to the priest, physically and spiritually in the offertory of the Mass. The priest accepts these gifts. And on behalf of the entire Church, he offers them to the Father in union with the perfect sacrifice of Christ on the cross.

Christ. Here, we discover that ultimately, the offertory of the Mass does not primarily answer the question, "What is being offered?" but rather, "Who is being offered [for consecration]?" And through the eyes of faith, with the light of reason, and expressed through the liturgy of the Mass, we come to discover that it is Christ, the High Priest, who presents himself as a victim to the Father. And because we are members of His Mystical Body through the sacrament of Baptism, we are also offering ourselves, presenting ourselves for sacrifice in

---

49   Code of Canon Law, 924.

union with Christ. As he freely sacrificed himself to the Father on the cross, so we are invited and encouraged to follow his perfect example. There we will find salvation. What is being offered in the offertory of the Mass? It is Christ, the head of the Church, in union with His Mystical Body, you and me. In the next lesson, we will continue our examination of the offertory by answering the following question: What is the purpose and the significance of the bread and wine used at the Mass?

16
Bread and Wine

W e have been examining the first movement of the Liturgy of the Eucharist, known as the offertory or preparation of the gifts. Clearly the most essential elements that are presented to the priest and offered for sacrifice are the bread and wine. Without bread and wine there is no Mass. Nothing may be substituted for these elements. What is so important about bread and wine? Why do we use bread and wine at every Mass?

Because the Church faithfully imitates Jesus Christ. At the Last Supper, the First Holy Mass, Jesus commanded his apostles, his college of bishops, "Do this in memory of me," thus giving them the power to offer the sacrifice of the Mass.[50] The Church faithfully follows the command of the Lord since she has no authority to change the essential elements of the sacrament. In the same way that Christ ordained men, his apostles, to be his priests, the Church may use only bread and wine for the sacrament of his Body and Blood.[51] The Church has the authority only to continue what Christ established. In instituting the sacrament on Holy Thursday, Jesus accepted the gifts presented at the Passover, namely, the bread and wine, blessed them, gave them to his apostles, and fulfilled the meaning of the Passover with his perfect sacrifice. Here, at the First Holy Mass, Our Lord delivered the blueprint for perfect worship, which necessitated the use of bread and wine. Therefore, the Church has legislated that bread and wine are essential, necessary to the Sacrifice of the Mass. What is so important about bread and wine?

At this point, we must penetrate a little deeper into the

---

50   Cf. *Catechism*, 1337.
51   Cf. *Catechism*, 1577.

mystery of the sacrament. To do this, we will inspect these two elements on four distinct levels: the natural, the symbolic, the theological, and the mystical/spiritual.

On the natural level, bread and wine have nourished mankind for centuries. They are common ingredients in the human diet almost since the beginning of time. It is natural that bread and wine would signify nourishment. On the symbolic level, both bread and wine symbolize the work of God and man—God provides the wheat and grapes, but man must labor to produce bread and wine. In order to manufacture bread, wheat is cultivated and harvested, sifted and ground into flour, added to water, kneaded and baked, before it can be used in the Mass. Likewise, wine is the end product resulting from the tending of grapes, harvesting them, crushing them, and fermenting the juice into a fine vintage. The process is time-consuming and laborious, symbolizing the cooperation of God and man, divine providence and human labor. On the theological level, bread and wine are first mentioned in the Book of Genesis in reference to the mysterious priest and king, Melchizedek. Melchizedek offered bread and wine as a gift pleasing to God.[52] His sacrifice foreshadowed the one, true, and perfect sacrifice of Jesus Christ, who is the definitive High Priest and King. Further, since many grains of wheat compose the bread and many grapes are crushed to produce wine, the bread and wine also theologically represent the Church, composed of many members. And on the mystical or spiritual level, since grains of wheat must be ground into flour and baked and grapes must be crushed into liquid and fermented, the actual process represents the agony, the suffering, and the passion of Christ that brought about our redemption. Wheat and grapes must undergo a kind of agony and passion in order to provide the elements of bread and wine. The natural, the

---

52   Genesis 14:18-20.

symbolic, the theological, and the mystical/spiritual levels all demonstrate that bread and wine are not only necessary, but appropriate elements to be used in the perfect sacrifice of Christ offered in an unbloody manner at each Holy Mass.

Next, let us return to the ritual of the Mass to examine the preparation of the altar and the offertory procession.

17
The Offertory Procession and Preparation

We have spent the past few lessons focusing on the significance of the Offertory. We discovered that ultimately Christ is offering himself as both the priest and victim of the sacrifice of the Mass. And since we are members of his Mystical Body, the Church, we are also offering ourselves with him. "Through him, with him, and in him," we offer ourselves as a gift to the Father. But before the offerings and gifts are consecrated, they must be collected and presented for sacrifice. Let us return to the ritual of the Liturgy of the Eucharist to see how this is accomplished.

At the beginning of the offertory, the altar is prepared. A square linen cloth, called the corporal, is unfolded in the center of the altar. The name "corporal" comes from the Latin corpus meaning "body," since this linen cloth is unfolded to catch particles of the host or drops of precious Blood. Along with the corporal, the chalice and communion chalices (if Communion is distributed under both species) are also brought to the altar with their purificators. The purificator is the linen cloth used to wipe and cleanse the chalices or other sacred vessels. Finally, the Roman Missal is placed on the altar.[53] The altar is now prepared to receive the gifts of bread and wine.

Earlier we recalled that the first action of the offertory is the collection. Here, the faithful have the opportunity to support the various material needs of the Church with their generous contributions. We also recognized that these donations not only support the needs of the Church,

---

53   GIRM, 73.

but purchase the bread and wine that are also presented. Ultimately, the collection symbolically represents ourselves: our work is compensated with money, from which a portion is given to God as a sacrificial offering. It is important to note that the bread and wine, along with the collection, is brought forward in procession by members of the faithful. In the early Church, the faithful would bring various gifts to be offered and presented at the offertory, including bread and wine, and other items for the poor, such as food, money, and clothing.[54] Since we live in a society where money is the basic mode of exchange, we generally limit these offerings to the essential gifts of bread and wine, along with the collection. Still, the ritual allows the presentation of other gifts that are "for the sake of charity toward the poor," but these must be placed away from the altar of sacrifice.[55] The gifts of bread and wine are accepted by the celebrant or deacon and carried to the altar with the assistance of servers. During the offertory collection and procession, the Offertory Hymn or chant may be sung by the choir or the congregation, at least until the gifts have been placed on the altar.[56]

As the gifts arrive at the altar, the celebrant raises the paten above the altar and offers a prayer in silence or, if there is no music, he may recite the prayer aloud. This prayer praises God for providing the elements for man to produce the bread used in the sacrifice. After this prayer, the celebrant places the paten and any ciboria with hosts on the corporal. The chalice is prepared by the deacon or, if there is no deacon, by the celebrant. He adds a drop of water into the wine and recites a prayer in silence: "By the mystery of this water and wine may we come to share in the divinity of Christ, who humbled himself to share in our humanity." It was common in ancient Roman society to drink wine mixed

---

54   *Understanding the Mass,* 109.
55   *Redemptionis Sacramentum,* 70.
56   GIRM, 74.

with water. This social practice entered the sacred rites of the Mass and assumed a spiritual significance: the wine represents the divinity of Christ and the water, his humanity. The mixture of wine and water also represents the mystery of divinization: the water represents man elevated by God.[57] After the chalice is prepared, it is elevated above the altar while another short prayer of praise is recited silently or aloud by the celebrant. He places the chalice and any communion chalices on the corporal and he may cover the chalice with a stiff square cloth, called the "pall." Of all the articles used in the Holy Sacrifice, the pall has perhaps the most practical function: to keep insects and other foreign elements out of the chalice. In the next lesson, we conclude our discussion of the Offertory rites.

---

57   Many Church Fathers taught that, "God became man that man might become God"

18
My Sacrifice and Yours

For the past several lessons, our catechesis on the Mass has focused on the first movement of the Liturgy of the Eucharist: the offertory. And we just discussed the preparation of the altar, the offertory procession of the gifts, and the offering prayers for the bread and the wine.

After the offering prayers are recited and the sacred vessels are placed on the square linen cloth, called the corporal, the celebrant bows to the altar and prays silently: "Lord God, we ask you to receive us and be pleased with the sacrifice we offer you with humble and contrite hearts." The priest speaks in his own name, as well as on behalf of the faithful, asking God to receive the gifts which he has just offered, namely, the gifts of bread and wine, as well as the sacrifice of ourselves. At this moment, the celebrant may place incense in the thurible, bless the incense, and incense the gifts, the altar, and the crucifix. This is now the third time that the incense may be used to signify the Church's offerings and prayers rising like incense in the sight of God. The incense unites the symbols of Christ: the altar, which is the central symbol in the sanctuary for Christ; the crucifix, which recalls the redemption that is re-presented in the Sacrifice of the Mass; and the bread and wine, which will actually become the Body and Blood of Christ in the consecration of the Mass. The incense may then be used to incense persons: first, the celebrant and then the concelebrants, by virtue of their sacred ministry as priests, then the faithful, by reason of their baptismal dignity, which grants them a share in the royal priesthood of Jesus Christ.[58]

After this third incensation, the celebrant then washes

---

58   *Catechism*, 1273.

his hands. What is the purpose of this gesture? Ritual purification is not a novel practice in the Holy Mass. Many ancient religions, in particular the Jews, maintained numerous traditional rites for the purification of vessels, as well as the hands of those who are partaking in the ritual itself. Further, in the early Church, it became practical necessity for the priest to wash his hands after the offertory. The faithful would present a vast array of offerings for the benefit of charity to the poor, including food, bread, vegetables, fruits, flasks of wine, and clothing. Following this extended offertory, it became necessary for the priest to purify his hands before touching the sacred vessels to offer the sacrifice. The ritual maintains its place in the Mass. Known as the lavabo rite, the washing of hands now refers more to an internal, spiritual purification, than an external one. As the celebrant is washing his hands, he recites a private prayer in silence to this effect: "Lord, wash away my iniquity; cleanse me from my sins." Notice that there is a distinction made between the iniquity that underlies the desire to sin, as well as the actual sins themselves. St. Cyril of Jerusalem comments on the mystical meaning of this ritual in the fourth century: "[The lavabo] shows that we must be free from all sin. We perform actions with our hands; to wash our hands is the nearest thing to purifying our deeds."[59]

The celebrant returns to the center of the altar and implores the faithful to unite themselves with him in the sacrifice that is drawing near. In the original Latin text, the priest says, "Orate, fratres: ut meum ac vestrum sacrificium..." ("Pray, brethren, that my sacrifice and yours...").[60] The prayer indicates the two distinct sacrifices of the Mass: Christ and his Body, the Church. Our current English translation simplifies this expression: "Pray, brethren, that our sacrifice...." The

---

59   *Understanding the Mass*, 115.
60   English translation: "Pray, brethren: that my sacrifice and yours..."

prayer is a sort of extended form of the more common "Let us pray." The people stand and respond, "May the Lord accept the sacrifice at your hands for the praise and glory of his name, for our good, and the good of all his Church." Finally, the "Prayer Over the Gifts" is the second proper collect or prayer of the Mass and signals the end of the offertory. This prayer usually acknowledges our inability to offer to God gifts adequate to his goodness and power. The Church prays that God will accept what we offer with sincerity and respond with generous graces as we prepare to enter the most solemn movement in the Mass: the consecration. In the next lesson, we will begin to examine the consecration as we move to the Eucharistic Prayer.

19
The Second Movement:
The Consecration

In our study of the Mass, we discovered that the Liturgy of the Eucharist is composed of three distinct movements: the offertory, the consecration, and the reception of Holy Communion. Last time, we concluded our examination of the offertory, where we have the opportunity to offer ourselves to God as Our Lord offered himself to his Heavenly Father. The essence of Christianity is the reproduction of what Jesus encountered in the soul of each and every individual in the world. As Our Lord accepted his suffering, crucifixion, death, and the glory of the resurrection, so also every person is to offer his or her human nature as an offering to the Heavenly Father. We are to die to sin in order to rise and live in grace and glory. In the offertory, we present and offer gifts of bread and wine as well as ourselves to the Father. And in the second movement, the consecration, we unite ourselves with the perfect sacrifice of Jesus Christ, the High Priest and Victim. We now turn to the second movement, the consecration, to investigate how this is accomplished.

The consecration of the Mass occurs within the larger context of the prayer, known as the Eucharistic Prayer or the Canon. The Eucharistic Prayer begins with the Preface and continues through the doxology chanted by the celebrant and concelebrants: "Through him, with him, and in him…." As a prayer of thanksgiving and sanctification, it is the center and the summit of the entire Mass.[61] The prayer is recited by the celebrant alone or parts may be recited by other concelebrating priests. In either case, the priest speaks

---

61   Cf. *Understanding the Mass,* 121.

on behalf of the Church, often denoted by the use of "we": "We offer to you..."; "We pray to you...."[62] However, in the "institution narrative," the person speaking changes, although the voice remains the same. No longer does the priest speak on behalf of the Church, but now Christ speaks. No longer is it "We pray to you...," but "This is my body." Here, within this prayer of the Son addressed to the Father, eternity punctures the time barrier, as the voice of Jesus Christ, the High Priest, is heard speaking the sacred words consecrating bread and wine into his own Body and Blood.[63] As Pope John Paul II wrote in Ecclesia de Eucharistia, "The priest says these words, or rather he puts his voice at the disposal of the One who spoke these words in the Upper Room and who desires that they should be repeated in every generation...".[64] This is the most solemn moment in the Mass; the greatest expression of love on earth. That is why the Church instructs us that "The Eucharistic Prayer demands that all listen to it with reverence and in silence".[65]

This second movement, known as the consecration, truly makes present the perfect sacrifice of Jesus Christ. As the Holy Father adds in the same encyclical, "When the Church celebrates the Eucharist, the memorial of her Lord's death and resurrection, this central event of salvation becomes really present and 'the work of our redemption is carried out.' ...The sacrifice of Christ and the sacrifice of the Eucharist are one single sacrifice".[66] And so before the Eucharist is a banquet, it is first of all the sacrifice of Our Lord on the cross. In other words, before the reception of Holy Communion is the consecration, where Christ perpetuates and continues throughout time his redemptive sacrifice. Why? What is

---

62   Roman Canon (Eucharistic Prayer I)
63   *Understanding the Mass,* 139.
64   *Ecclesia de Eucharistia,* 5.
65   GIRM, 78.
66   *Ecclesia de Eucharistia,* 11.

the purpose of continually re-presenting his sacrifice if the redemption already occurred?

Above all, the sacrifice of Christ is true worship of the Father. The sacrifice of the Son gives glory and honor to the Father. Further, you and I are the beneficiaries of his sacrifice. The fruits of the redemption must now be applied to our souls. Finally, Jesus instructed us to, "Do this in memory of me." And so in humble obedience, the Church faithfully follows the command of the Lord to offer the sacrifice of Christ, that not only may bread and wine become his Body and Blood, but more importantly, that we may be consecrated to him and more and more become what we receive: the Body of Christ.

20
Sanctus, Sanctus, Sanctus

We already began our investigation of the Eucharistic Prayer, which begins the second movement of the Liturgy of the Eucharist, known as the consecration. In the consecration, we unite ourselves with the perfect sacrifice of Jesus Christ, the High Priest and Victim and thereby render true worship to the Father and receive the fruit of our redemption. Let us continue with our study of the Eucharistic Prayer to trace the elements that unfold this mystery of our salvation.

Since the advent of the Novus Ordo (New Mass) authorized by Pope Paul VI after the Second Vatican Council, there are several options for the Eucharistic Prayer of the Mass given in the Roman Missal: four common Eucharistic Prayers, three prayers that may be used for Masses with children, and two that may be used for Masses of Reconciliation, as well as other approved prayers. Of the four main Eucharistic Prayers, the first Eucharistic Prayer, commonly known as the Roman Canon, originated in Rome at the end of the fourth century.[67] It developed its present form around the seventh century and has had no significant changes since.[68] In fact, the Roman Canon was the only Canon used exclusively in the Roman Rite since the Council of Trent until the Second Vatican Council (1563-1965). This Prayer contains two lists of saints: the first includes the apostles and the early Popes, while the second list includes many early martyrs. The second Eucharistic Prayer is the shortest and is similar to the text of St. Hippolytus dated around the year 215.[69] The third Eucharistic Prayer is a reconfiguration of the Roman Canon,

---

67   *Understanding the Mass,* 126.
68   *Ibid.*
69   *Ibid.*

rich with Eastern influences and emphasizes the work of the Holy Spirit. Finally, the fourth Eucharistic Prayer provides a fuller summary of salvation history and relies extensively on Biblical events and is in the great tradition of Eucharistic Prayers from the East, most notably from St. Basil.

Within the variety of Eucharistic Prayers, there are certain commonalities that define them as Eucharistic Prayers. The Eucharistic Prayer is composed of several parts that can be distinguished as follows: a) Thanksgiving (Preface), b) Acclamation (Sanctus), c) Epiclesis, d) Institution Narrative and Consecration, e) Anamnesis (Memorial), f) Offering, g) Intercessions, and h) the final doxology.[70] The Eucharistic Prayer actually begins with the Preface and its customary dialogue between the celebrant and the congregation. Ever since the third century, this series of three verses and responses has marked the introduction of the Preface.[71] Here is established the ultimate purpose of the Mass introduced in our first lesson: Dignum et iustum est ("It is right and just").[72] Immediately following this dialogue is the first part of the Eucharistic Prayer we mentioned a moment ago: Thanksgiving. As with the Eucharistic Prayers, there is a variety of Prefaces found in the Roman Rite that change depending upon the festival of the day or the liturgical season of the year. The Preface expresses profound praise and gratitude to the Father for the wonders of his creation and the wonderful work of redemption accomplished by his divine Son. Each preface concludes by singing the unending hymn of praise, called the Sanctus (Sanctus is the first Latin word, which means "Holy").

The Sanctus is sung by all and is the second part of the Eucharistic Prayer. What is the origin of this mysterious hymn? The Sanctus was added to the Mass by Pope St.

---

70   GIRM, 79.
71   *Understanding the Mass*, 128.
72   Please refer to lesson 1 for a fuller explanation of this idea.

Sixtus (119-128).[73] This hymn is composed of two parts. The first part, "Holy, holy, holy Lord God of power and might, heaven and earth are full of your glory," is taken from the vision of the Prophet Isaiah (6:1-3), where he saw the Lord sitting upon the throne surrounded by angels singing this hymn. The second part, "Blessed is he who comes in the name of the Lord. Hosanna in the highest," is taken from the shouts of praise offered to Jesus as he made his triumphant entry into Jerusalem, which we commemorate on Palm Sunday (Matthew 21:9). In the Sanctus, we unite ourselves to the angelic voices of heaven as we draw near to the Divine Throne and await the coming of Our Savior. The Sanctus is the final warning of the immanent approach of Our Lord, who will become truly present in a few moments in the consecration. With haste we unite our voices with the heavenly host of angels and saints and await Our Savior's coming. The next presentation will continue with our examination of the Epiclesis and the Institution Narrative and Consecration.

---

73   *Understanding the Mass*, 134.

21
This Is My Body

In these reflections on the Mass, we have examined the first two parts of the Eucharistic Prayer: the Preface and the Sanctus. As soon as the Sanctus comes to completion, the faithful assume the posture of kneeling in humble adoration, awaiting the King of Kings, before whom "every knee must bend".[74] Then, with the simplicity of one lone voice breaking the silence of the Upper Room at the Last Supper, Jesus Christ, the High Priest, utters the sacred words through his priest, the words that he donated to His Church on Holy Thursday. Through this divine mystery, bread and wine actually change into the Body and Blood, Soul and Divinity of Jesus Christ, leaving behind only the appearances of bread and wine.

We could admittedly spend months studying and contemplating this divine mystery that lies at the heart of the Mass. But for the sake of brevity and clarity, let us focus our attention only on what pertains to this mystery of faith: the words and actions that effect this sacrament. To investigate how this is accomplished, we must now turn to the next two parts of the Eucharistic Prayer: the epiclesis and the institution narrative and consecration.

The word epiclesis is a Greek composite of two words: kaleo, meaning "to call, summon, or invite," and when preceded by the preposition epi, the word means, "to call down." During this third part of the Eucharistic Prayer, the priest "calls down" the Holy Spirit and signifies this activity by placing his hands over the gifts that are to be sacrificed. Sanctuary bells may be rung at this time to call our attention.[75]

---

74   GIRM, 43; cf. Phil 2:10.
75   GIRM, 150.

The epiclesis has at least two main spiritual meanings: 1) In the Old Testament Temple sacrifices, the priest would place his hands on the lamb of sacrifice, dedicating it for sacrifice; 2) also, the epiclesis recalls the mystery of the Incarnation, where the Holy Spirit descended upon and overshadowed the Blessed Virgin Mary so that the Word became flesh.[76] Indeed, the Holy Sacrifice of the Mass unites these two mysteries together as Jesus Christ becomes both priest and victim of the sacrifice and again comes to us sacramentally in the flesh, which now brings us to the fourth part of the Eucharistic Prayer.

During the institution narrative and the consecration, the familiar voice of Jesus Christ is heard as the High Priest of every sacrifice of the Mass. Each priest lends himself to the service of Christ, so that Our Lord can once again re-present his sacrifice. It is not simply the priest who speaks, "This is my body," since it is not his body, per se, but rather it is Christ who speaks, "This is my body…this is my blood." These words actually effect the change from bread and wine into the Body and Blood, Soul and Divinity of Christ. Just as Christ took bread and wine at the Last Supper, blessed it, and gave it to his apostles after he consecrated it into his Body and Blood, he continues to offer them for our salvation. This change from bread and wine into the Body and Blood of Christ is known as transubstantiation, meaning a "change in substance."[77] The whole substance of bread and wine is changed into the substance of Christ's Body and Blood. The accidents or the appearances of bread and wine remain the same. Therefore, when we receive the Holy Eucharist, we do not receive bread and wine with the Body and Blood of Christ (consubstantiation); we do not receive bread and wine that merely signifies the Body and Blood of Christ

76   Cf. Lev. 16:21-22; Luke 1:35.
77   Cf. *Ecclesia de Eucharistia,* 15; *Catechism,* 1376.

(transignification; transfinalization); on the contrary, we do receive the Body and Blood of Christ, the same crucified, risen, and glorified body of Christ, under the appearances of bread and wine. Christ said, "This is my body." We have no reason to doubt him, who is incapable of deceiving us. The consecration actually occurs in two distinct consecrations: first the body, then the blood, signifying the death of Christ, whose precious blood was separated from his body on the cross. After each consecration is a moment of adoration, a sacred moment in which the Body and Blood of Christ may be incensed (the fourth and final incensation), a sacred moment which prepares us for that moment of divine intimacy whereby God desires to enter divine communion with us.[78] We will continue with the Eucharistic Prayer in the next consideration.

---

78   GIRM, 150.

22
Mysterium Fidei

Last time, we examined the sacred words of institution and consecration, which constitute the heart of the Holy Sacrifice of the Mass. We discovered the amazing truth that these are not merely historical or Biblical words used to recount the activity of the Last Supper, but in fact, in the Holy Mass, Christ truly re-presents his sacrifice through his priest acting as his instrument. Bread and wine are changed into the Body and Blood of Christ as the words of consecration are spoken by Christ through each individual Catholic priest throughout time and history. All the prayers of the Mass until this moment prepare for Our Lord's sacramental arrival; from this moment forward, when Christ is truly present on the altar, the priest again addresses the Heavenly Father on behalf of the Church. Now let us consider the four remaining parts of the Eucharistic Prayer that are now addressed to the Father.

Anamnesis. Immediately following the consecration, the celebrant announces: "Let us proclaim the mystery of faith," ("Mysterium fidei" in the Latin) and we respond with one of the four options that expresses the Paschal Mystery: "Dying you destroyed our death. Rising you restored our life. Lord Jesus, come in glory." This acclamation leads us into the next part of the Eucharistic Prayer, called by its Greek name, anamnesis, or "memorial." The anamnesis is a prayer of remembrance in which the Church calls to mind the Lord's passion, resurrection, and ascension into heaven. We are reminded that the Church is acting in memory of Our Lord and obeying his explicit command, "Do this in memory of me." We are mindful of Our Lord's parting mandate and the Church rejoices in her fidelity to Christ; we are, in fact, faithfully following the command to "Do this in memory of me."

Oblation. The oblation or offering follows the memorial in the Eucharistic Prayer. Prior to the consecration, the priest asks the Lord to accept the gifts of bread and wine as a token of ourselves. But now, following the consecration, the bread and wine no longer exist; they have been changed into the Body and Blood of the risen Christ. Christ is now offered to the Father. In the Roman Canon, three Old Testament persons are mentioned whose offerings were acceptable to the Father: 1) Abel, who offered the firstborn lamb of his flock, 2) Abraham, who was willing to offer his own son, and 3) Melchisedech, who offered bread and wine as a priest of God.[79] Each of these three Biblical sacrifices foreshadows the perfect sacrifice of Jesus Christ, which fulfilled all others. Christ is the High priest offering the Mass, but in the oblation, we discover that he is also the Victim being offered.

Intercessions. Because Christ is the High Priest and mediator between God and man, intercessory prayers form the next part of the Eucharistic Prayer. The intercessions make clear that each Holy Mass is offered for the salvation of the whole world in union with the entire Church on earth, as well as in heaven. All members of Christ's Mystical Body are included in the benefits of the Mass: we seek the intercession of those in heaven, the Blessed Virgin Mary and all the angels and saints; we pray for the living and we intercede on behalf of the dead. The pope, the bishop of the diocese, and the clergy are always mentioned, since union with the pope and the local bishop establishes our unity with the Catholic Church throughout the world.

Doxology. With the close of the intercessions comes the conclusion of the Eucharistic Prayer. The formula, known as the Doxology, is common to all Eucharistic Prayers. The

---

79   Genesis 4:4, 14:17-20 (Cf. Hebrews 7), 22:1-19.

Greek word doxology simply means "A word of glory or praise." The priest raises the chalice and paten in a final word of praise to the Father as he prays, "Through him, with him, in him, in the unity of the Holy Spirit, all glory and honor is yours Almighty Father, forever and ever." The faithful conclude the Eucharistic Prayer with the "Amen," which may be recited or sung. St. Jerome wrote in the 5th century that the "Amen" at the conclusion of the Eucharistic Prayer "resounded in heaven, as a celestial thunderclap in the Roman basilicas."[80] Let us pray that our assent, that our "Amen," will proceed from the same ardent faith, hope, and love. Next, we will continue by examining the Communion Rite.

---

80   *Understanding the Mass*, 163.

23
Third Movement: Communion

As we began our discussion of the Liturgy of the Eucharist, we discovered that the drama of our redemption is unfolded in three movements during the Holy Sacrifice of the Mass: the offertory, the consecration, and the reception of Holy Communion. In the offertory, not only are bread and wine presented and offered, but more importantly, we offer ourselves to the Father along with Christ who offers himself. In the offertory we present ourselves for sacrifice with Christ; in the consecration we die with him. We apply his death to ourselves that we may share his resurrection and glory. And in Holy Communion, we find that we have not died, but that we have come to life. In a certain sense, the substance of bread and wine must be sacrificed, must cease to exist, so that it may become the Body and Blood of Christ. In the same way, our old habits of sin must also be sacrificed so that we might have new life in Christ. Let us now turn to the Communion Rite to inspect this third movement of the Liturgy of the Eucharist.

The Communion Rite begins at the conclusion of the Eucharistic Prayer. The faithful now stand and, at the invitation of the celebrant, sing or recite the Lord's Prayer. It is important to note that there is no instruction in the Roman Missal to join hands during this prayer or during any prayer of the Mass.[81]

From the most ancient historical documents and records of theologians and saints, the Lord's Prayer was included in the Mass prior to receiving Holy Communion.[82] It is fitting that this prayer is placed between the Eucharistic Prayer and

---

81 Cf. GIRM, 81.
82 *Understanding the Mass,* 169ff.

reception of Holy Communion since: 1) the seven petitions of the Lord's Prayer summarize the petitions offered in the Eucharistic Prayer and 2) the Lord's Prayer is the proper prayer of the whole Church, uniting and preparing the faithful for divine communion.[83] In the Mass, the celebrant invites us to pray to our heavenly Father with filial boldness, since it was Jesus, the Son of God, who taught us to call God "Our Father." Through the sacrament of Baptism, we have truly become adopted sons and daughters of the heavenly Father through his Son. Therefore, when "we pray to the Father, we are in communion with him and with his Son, Jesus Christ.[84] But this communion is a spiritual communion, one which prepares us for the sacramental communion that will occur when we receive the Holy Eucharist.

From early on, reciting the Lord's Prayer in the Mass contained a unique conclusion. The Didache and the Apostolic Constitutions added a doxology to the end of the Lord's Prayer. This practice is retained in the Mass, but the final doxology follows a prayer recited by the celebrant, known as the embolism, meaning "extension." Developing the final petition of the Lord's Prayer, the celebrant prays for deliverance from evil for the entire community of the faithful and ends with the hope of the Second Coming of our Lord Jesus Christ.

The short ritual known as the Rite of Peace follows the Lord's Prayer and is introduced by the celebrant with a prayer directed to Jesus Christ, who is truly present on the altar. This prayer recalls the gift of the risen Christ to his apostles on the day of his glorious resurrection and expresses ecclesial communion and mutual charity before receiving Holy Communion.[85] The deacon or priest may invite us to

---

83   Cf. *Catechism,* 2770.
84   *Catechism,* 2781.
85   John 20:19ff; GIRM, 82.

exchange the sign of peace with those nearest to us. The priest and ministers are not normally allowed to leave the sanctuary to exchange the sign of peace, since the priest has already exchanged peace with the faithful.[86] Ultimately, what we discover as we approach Holy Communion is that our communion with another (in faith, as well as charity) is to be established before it is to be expressed by receiving Communion. We will continue with preparations for Holy Communion in the next lesson.

---

86   GIRM, 82; *Redemptionis Sacramentum,* 72.

24
Ecce Agnus Dei

In the past few lessons, we have been discussing several short rites that make up the Communion Rite. Thus far we have inspected the Lord's Prayer and the Rite of Peace. Let us now finish our examination of these rites that prepare and dispose us to receive Holy Communion.

Following the Rite of Peace is a subtle, yet highly significant act called the Fraction Rite. The celebrant, following the example of Our Lord, now takes up the consecrated host and reverently breaks it. Although this action is accomplished without drama or commentary, it bears great significance in the history and tradition of the Mass.[87] All of the sacred writers of the New Testament affirm that Christ took bread and broke it when he offered the sacrifice of the Last Supper. After his resurrection, he was recognized by his disciples "in the breaking of the bread".[88] And the Acts of the Apostles testifies that the early Church continued "the breaking of the bread" faithfully each day.[89] To the present day, the Church continues "the breaking of the bread" precisely because Christ the Lord instructed his Apostles to "Do this in memory of me." But why does Our Lord break the bread?

Certainly it was Jewish custom to break bread with one's relatives and friends as an act of charity. And ancient custom dictated that breaking bread was appropriate rather than slicing or cutting it with a knife. But perhaps more important is the spiritual significance of breaking the bread that not only represented Christ's body, but sacramentally becomes his body, which was pierced and nailed to the cross.

---

87   Cf. *Redemptionis Sacramentum,* 73.
88   Luke 24:35
89   Acts 2:46

A fragment of the broken host is then placed into the chalice, a gesture called "the commingling." The origin of this custom is not certain, but there are a number of possible explanations. Centuries ago there was the custom of taking pieces of the consecrated host from the Mass offered by the bishop of a diocese and distributing them to the various parishes in his diocese. The priest would then place the fragment into his chalice signifying unity with the local bishop.[90] It is also probable that this commingling of the Body and Blood of Christ has a more spiritual explanation. The consecration of the Mass occurs in two separate consecrations: first the bread, then the wine. Since this separate consecration symbolically represents death, as Our Lord's blood was separated from his body, uniting and commingling the Body and Blood of Christ in the chalice would symbolically represent the resurrection, the re-union of Christ's Body and Blood.[91] The celebrant recites a prayer in silence during this commingling: "May this mingling of the body and blood of our Lord Jesus Christ bring eternal life to us who receive it."

Meanwhile, the Agnus Dei is recited or sung. At first, the breaking of the bread was done in silence. But in the seventh century, Pope St. Sergius established the chanting of this hymn, which had been familiar to him since his childhood.[92] The Agnus Dei or "Lamb of God" as a title of Our Lord is most appropriate at this point in the Mass. In the Old Testament, the "lamb of God" was slaughtered for the Passover feast and saved the Israelites from the angel of death.[93] St. John the Baptist saw Jesus walking toward him on the banks of the river Jordan and said, "Behold, the

---

90   *The Mass,* 368ff.
91   *Understanding the Mass,* 179-180.
92   *Ibid.,* 180.
93   Exodus 12.

Lamb of God, who takes away the sin of the world!"[94] And the evangelist, St. John, recorded his visions in the Book of Revelation of the slain Lamb, Jesus Christ, who was glorious and victorious in heaven.[95] After the priest has completed his private preparatory prayers, he genuflects and raises the host above the paten or chalice and recites the words of St. John the Baptist, "This is the Lamb of God who takes away the sins of the world. Happy are those who are called to his supper."[96] We must pause for a moment, look, adore, and behold him, who alone takes away the sins of the world. It is not mere bread or symbol, but the same Lord who once walked along the banks of the river Jordan. Indeed, "Happy are those who are called to his supper."[97]

---

94   John 1:29
95   Revelation 14ff
96   *"Ecce Agnus Dei, ecce qui tollit peccata mundi. Beati qui ad cenam Agni vocati sunt."* [A more precise English translation could be rendered, "Behold the Lamb of God, behold him who takes away the sins of the world. Blessed are those who are called to the banquet of the Lamb."]
97   Revelation 19:9

25
Domine, Non Sum Dignus

In our last discussion, we examined the rituals that prepare and dispose us to receive Holy Communion. As a final act of preparation, the celebrant raises the host above the paten or chalice and recites the words of St. John the Baptist: "This is the Lamb of God who takes away the sins of the world." All respond with the words of the Centurion soldier from the Gospel: "Lord, I am not worthy to receive you, but only say the word and I shall be healed" (in the current English translation).[98] This final act of humility and trust is not only the most appropriate preparation for Holy Communion but the best perspective to approach our discussion: "Lord, I am not worthy."

No one is worthy, per se, to receive the most sublime gift of the Church's treasury, namely, Christ himself. It is only necessary that the priest receive Holy Communion at the Mass for the sacrifice to be complete and the Mass to be offered validly. However, the Church has encouraged the faithful to receive Holy Communion, so that they too might partake of the innumerable spiritual graces and benefits of the Holy Eucharist. The Church even mandates the faithful to receive Holy Communion at least once a year during the Easter season.[99] But who is allowed to receive Holy Communion?

According to Canon Law, "Any baptized person not prohibited by law can and must be admitted to Holy

---

98   Matthew 8:8; *"Domine, non sum dignus, ut intres sub tectum meum, sed tantum dic verbo et sanabitur anima mea"* [A more precise English translation could be rendered, "Lord, I am not worthy that you should enter under my roof, but only say the word and my soul shall be healed."]
99   *Code of Canon Law,* 920.

Communion".[100] Those prohibited by law would include those not in communion with the Catholic Church, children under the age of reason, those who persevere in manifest grave sin, etc. For those who are not permitted to receive Holy Communion, it should be noted that they are not excluded from the worship of God by attending Mass and they should be encouraged to make a "spiritual communion" while others are receiving Communion. A spiritual communion is the traditional practice of uniting oneself to Christ in a prayer of self-offering that seeks to receive the graces and benefits of Christ's sacrifice.[101]

Returning to the Communion Rite of the Mass, the priest receives the consecrated host after saying silently, "May the Body of Christ bring me to everlasting life." Similarly, he receives the Precious Blood after saying silently, "May the Blood of Christ bring me to everlasting life." At this point, the celebrant may be assisted by other ordinary ministers of Holy Communion, such as concelebrating priests or deacons. If there are not enough ordinary ministers to distribute Holy Communion, extraordinary ministers now approach the altar to receive Communion and assist the priest.[102] After the celebrant has received Communion, the Communion antiphon is recited or the Communion chant begins. The purpose of the hymn is to express unity of voices and joy of heart while the faithful begin the communion procession, the second principal procession of the Holy Mass.[103]

As the faithful approach the minister to receive Holy Communion, the communicant is to make a sign of reverence before receiving. The general norm in the United States is to bow before the Blessed Sacrament and to bow again before

---

100 *Ibid.,* 912.
101 See Appendix D for a Suggested Prayer for Receiving a Spiritual
     Communion
102 *Redemptionis Sacramentum,* 88.
103 GIRM, 86.

the chalice containing the Precious Blood. The minister shows the consecrated host to the communicant and says, "The Body of Christ"; likewise, the minister presents the chalice with Precious Blood and says, "The Blood of Christ." The communicant makes the sign of reverence and responds, "Amen," meaning, "I believe" or "So be it." This response is simple, yet essential. It is an act of faith that, indeed, the communicant is fully aware that he or she is about to receive the true Body and Blood of Christ. After the reception of Holy Communion, the priest places the remaining hosts in the tabernacle and purifies the sacred vessels at the altar or credence table.[104] At this time, it is highly recommended to observe a few moments of silence, since the Body and Blood of the Lord is truly present in the body and soul of each communicant. These are the most precious moments on earth. "Domine, non sum dignus, Lord, I am not worthy" and yet, he continues to "welcome sinners and eat with them".[105] After a few moments of silence, the celebrant stands and invites the faithful to pray: "Let us pray." The Communion Rite closes with the third proper collect or prayer of the Mass, known as the "Prayer after Communion." In the next lesson, we will examine the Concluding Rites of the Mass.

---

104   GIRM, 278-280.
105   Cf. Matthew 9:11

26
Ite, Missa Est

In our discussion of the Communion Rite last time, we concluded by mentioning that the "Prayer After Communion" completes the Communion Rite. Following the Communion Rite is a decidedly short and simple conclusion to the Mass, called the "Concluding Rite," consisting of relatively few parts. Let us now examine how the Mass is ended by investigating these parts.

The ritual of the Mass allows a time and a place for announcements that are to be given after the "Prayer After Communion." There are two specifications for these announcements: they are to be brief and necessary.[106] The priest then greets the faithful in the usual manner, "The Lord be with you," with its usual response by the faithful. The celebrant then blesses the faithful with the customary sign of the cross and invocation of the Holy Trinity. He concludes the Mass in the same manner in which it was initiated; the prayer of the Mass, the highest form of prayer known to mankind, is now completed with the Trinitarian blessing. On solemn feasts and special occasions, there may be a more elaborate prayer over the people, which is usually begun with the instruction by the deacon or celebrant, "Bow your heads and pray for God's blessing."

One final exchange remains between the deacon, or if there is no deacon, the celebrant, and the faithful, known as the "Dismissal." The deacon says, "The Mass is ended, go in peace," "Go in the peace of Christ," or "Go in peace to love and serve the Lord."[107] The faithful respond one last time, "Thanks be to God" ("Deo Gratias"). The dismissal,

---

106 GIRM, 90.
107 *"Ite, missa est."* [A more precise English translation could be rendered, "Go, it is the dismissal."]

although very subtle and concise, holds great theological importance. It is the dismissal that gives the Mass its name: "the Mass" comes from the Latin word Missa, meaning "sent" or "dismissed." The faithful go to Mass, not merely as an escape from the world or as a diversion from one's Christian responsibilities, but rather that they might be sent back into the world, fortified by the grace of God. Having rendered to God the worship of the Holy Sacrifice of the Mass and having received the fruits of redemption, the faithful can better accomplish the duties of their particular vocation in the midst of the world, to sanctify the home, the workplace, the school, the marketplace, etc.

But before the celebrant and the faithful depart, the celebrant and deacon reverence the altar once again with a kiss and either bow to the altar or, if the tabernacle is in the sanctuary, they genuflect to the reserved Sacrament in the tabernacle. There may be a recessional hymn that accompanies the movement of the ministers from the sanctuary, but this is not necessary since the Mass is already ended. Now what?

Immediately upon the completion of Mass, it has been recommended by the Church for centuries to remain for a time of personal thanksgiving. We are encouraged to remain quiet, kneel down, and thank God for the outpouring of grace and mercy received in Holy Communion.[108] St. José Maria Escrivá advises us, "Do not leave the Church almost immediately after receiving the sacrament. Surely you have nothing so important to attend to that you cannot give Our Lord ten minutes to say thanks…. Love is paid for with love."[109]

Perhaps you had the experience of watching the film "The Passion of the Christ" in the theatre. What was the response of the audience to the powerful events of the Lord's passion, crucifixion, death, and resurrection? Each of the four times

---

108 See Appendix C for Suggested Prayers after the Holy Sacrifice of the Mass
109 *Understanding the Mass*, 201.

I saw the film in the theatre elicited the same response from the audience: silence, stillness, awe. The Mass is the same powerful, dramatic, bloody sacrifice re-presented in an unbloody manner. If we had the grace to better understand the mystery of the Mass, I dare suggest that we would also discover the same reaction in our souls: silence, stillness, adoration, and thanksgiving. Next time, we will finish our series, "Understanding the Mystery of the Mass" with a short review and a few concluding remarks.

27
A Pledge of Future Glory

For the past 26 lessons we have examined and discussed the constitutive parts of the Holy Sacrifice of the Mass. We have focused our attention on the basic structure, historical, theological and spiritual significance of each of these parts. However, a study such as the one we just completed that attempts to dissect its subject may leave the audience with the impression that the Mass is a loose compilation of dissimilar parts. Therefore, it is necessary to reiterate the essential coherence of the Holy Mass as one single act of worship, a reality that we mentioned from the beginning.

Indeed, from beginning to end, with all its parts, the Holy Sacrifice of the Mass is the prayer of self-sacrifice and thanksgiving of the eternal Son offered to the eternal Father, in which we, as his Mystical Body, render to God worship, adoration, praise, and thanksgiving. In each Mass, we unite ourselves with the worship of Jesus Christ, the High Priest and Victim, unto the Father in the Holy Spirit. By recalling the events of Christ's passion, death, and resurrection at every Mass, we are truly present at Calvary, when Christ presented himself and offered the one perfect sacrifice of his Body and Blood to the Father, thereby offering the fruits of his sacrifice to his bride, the Church. Consequently, the Mass provides us access to the saving mysteries of our faith: the events of the past are brought into the present that the benefits of our redemption may be applied to our souls. Therefore, the past 26 lessons of the Mass have principally dealt with examining the events of the past that are brought into the present at each Holy Mass. But what about the future? Indeed, there is still a further explanation that is necessary, a further aspect of the Mass not yet investigated: the eschatological reality, the final

79

end toward which the Holy Sacrifice of the Mass is directed.

In his encyclical on the Holy Eucharist, entitled, Ecclesia de Eucharistia, Pope John Paul II of happy memory discusses the eschatological reality of the Mass:

> The Eucharist is a straining toward the goal, a foretaste of the fullness of joy promised by Christ (Cf. John 15:11); it is in some way the anticipation of heaven, the "pledge of future glory." In the Eucharist, everything speaks of confident waiting 'in joyful hope for the coming of our Savior, Jesus Christ'.[110]

And not only does the Holy Eucharist anticipate future glory, but the Holy Father explains that in the Mass, our bond of communion with the Church already in heaven is strengthened, that we actually participate in the heavenly liturgy:

> The eschatological tension kindled by the Eucharist expresses and reinforces our communion with the Church in heaven.... This is an aspect of the Eucharist which merits greater attention: in celebrating the sacrifice of the Lamb, we are united to the heavenly "liturgy" and become part of that great multitude which cries out: "Salvation belongs to our God who sits upon the throne, and to the Lamb!" (Rev. 7:10). The Eucharist is truly a glimpse of heaven appearing on earth. It is a glorious ray of the heavenly Jerusalem which pierces the clouds of our history and lights up our journey.[111]

Therefore, our participation in the Holy Sacrifice of the Mass anticipates and prepares us for our eternal occupation in heaven, of offering praise, glory, adoration, and worship to

---

110 *Ecclesia de Eucharistia*, 18.
111 *Ibid.*, 19.

the Father with the Son in the Holy Spirit. And "as we wait in joyful hope for the coming of Our Savior," the advent of his promised return in glory, the Church orients herself to the east, the land of the rising sun, and faithfully continues to "Do this in memory of me"; the mystery of the Mass is thus re-presented on every altar in every Catholic Church throughout time and history, so that we may unite ourselves to the mystery of divine love, which impelled St. Thomas Aquinas to exclaim: "O Sacred Banquet, in which Christ becomes our food, the memory of his passion is celebrated, the soul is filled with grace, and a pledge of future glory is given to us."[112]

In the end, we have come to discover that "Understanding the Mystery of the Mass" is not merely an academic exercise, but a profound spiritual joy as we recognize the truth of Adrienne von Speyr's initial claim that, "The Holy Mass is both the means and the sign through which the Lord bequeaths us his love."

---

112 *Catechism,* 1402.

Appendix A:
The Holy Hour:
"Could You Not Keep Watch
For One Hour?"

On the night that Jesus Christ offered the Last Supper, the First Holy Mass, on the night that Our Lord instituted the sacrament of the Holy Eucharist, the sacrament that would fulfill his promise and desire to be with us always, until the end of the world, he escorted his apostles into the Garden of Gethsemane for a time of watching and prayer. As he was communing with the Eternal Father in prayer and in agony, his apostles were fast asleep. On three occasions, Our Lord returned to find his weary disciples asleep. He therefore posed this question to them, the perennial question that has echoed throughout the centuries and has revisited his disciples in every age: "Could you not keep watch for one hour?"[113]

Why should I make a holy hour? Why should I spend time in adoration of the Blessed Sacrament? What benefits await me if I sacrifice an hour of my time each day, each week?

Beloved Archbishop Fulton J. Sheen (1895-1979), who was renowned for his ability not only to spend an hour each day in the presence of Our Lord in the Blessed Sacrament (over 60 years of his life), but also his evangelization of others to do the same, wrote frequently about the fruits and effects of making a Holy Hour each day. His autobiography, "Treasure in Clay," reveals in chapter 12 entitled, "The Hour That Makes My Day," his ardent love and devotion for spending time with Our Lord each day. He writes, "The purpose of the Holy Hour is to encourage deep personal encounter with Christ. The holy and glorious God is constantly inviting us to come to Him,

---

113 Mark 14:37

to hold converse with Him, to ask for such things as we need and to experience what a blessing there is in fellowship with Him".[114]

In another book by the Archbishop, entitled, "The Priest Is Not His Own," Sheen delivers a comprehensive list of benefits of the Holy Hour that is worth repeating. Since his book is written particularly for priests, let us shorten his list of 15 Reasons to Make a Holy Hour to the following 10 reasons that all of us, clergy and laity alike, should enjoy a Holy Hour (daily or at least on a weekly basis). To the question, "Why make a Holy Hour," Bishop Sheen gives the following responses:

1. Because it is time spent in the Presence of Our Lord Himself. If faith is alive, no further reason is needed.
2. Because in our busy life it takes considerable time to shake off the... worldly cares that cling to our souls like dust.
3. Because Our Lord asked for it. [See explanation above—Mark 14:37]
4. Because the Holy Hour keeps a balance between the spiritual and the practical. The Holy Hour unites the contemplative life to the active life; it is Martha walking with Mary.
5. Because the Holy Hour makes us obedient instruments of God.
6. Because the Holy Hour helps us make reparation both for the sins of the world and for our own sins.
7. Because it will restore our lost spiritual vitality. Our hearts will be where our joys are.
8. Because the Holy Hour is the hour of truth. Alone with Jesus, we there see ourselves not as others see us, but as the Judge sees us.

---

114 Fulton J. Sheen, *Treasure in Clay* (San Francisco: Ignatius Press: 1993), 190.

9. Because it reduces our liability to temptation and weakness.

10. Because the Holy Hour is personal prayer. The Holy Mass and the Rosary are formal, official prayers, belonging to the Mystical Body of Christ. They do not belong to us personally. But the Holy Hour provides opportunity for personal discourse.

Ultimately, love is never forced and we are never coerced into spending time with the Lord. That is why "on the night he was betrayed," on the night Our Lord instituted the Holy Eucharist, he invited his disciples as he invites us today, "Could you not keep watch for one hour?"

Appendix B:
Suggested Prayers in Preparation for
The Holy Sacrifice of the Mass

Prayer of St. Thomas Aquinas (1225-1274)

Almighty and ever-living God, I approach the sacrament of your only-begotten Son, our Lord Jesus Christ. I come sick to the doctor of life, unclean to the fountain of mercy, blind to the radiance of eternal light, and poor and needy to the Lord of heaven and earth. Lord, in your great generosity, heal my sickness, wash away my defilement, enlighten my blindness, enrich my poverty, and clothe my nakedness. May I receive the bread of angels, the King of kings and Lord of lords, with humble reverence, with the purity and faith, the repentance and love, and the determined purpose that will help to bring me to salvation. May I receive the sacrament of the Lord's Body and Blood, and its reality and power. Kind God, may I receive the Body of your only-begotten Son, our Lord Jesus Christ, born from the womb of the Virgin Mary, and so be received into his Mystical Body and numbered among his members. Loving Father, as on my earthly pilgrimage I now receive your beloved Son under the veil of a sacrament, may I one day see him face to face in glory, who lives and reigns with you forever and ever. Amen.

Preparation for Holy Communion

O Lord, Jesus Christ, King of everlasting glory, behold I desire to come to you this day, and to receive your Body and Blood in this heavenly Sacrament, for your honor and glory, and the good of my soul. I desire to receive you, because it is your desire, and you have so willed it: blessed be your Name forever. I desire to come to you like Magdalen, that I may be delivered from all my evils, and embrace you, my only Good. I desire to come to you, that I may be happily united to you, that I may henceforth abide in you, and you in me; and that nothing in life or death may ever separate me from you. Amen.

Prayer before Holy Communion
From the Byzantine Liturgy

O Lord, I believe and profess that you are truly Christ, the Son of the living God, who came into the world to save sinners, of whom I am the first. Accept me as a partaker of your mystical supper, O Son of God; for I will not reveal your mystery to your enemies, nor will I give you a kiss as did Judas, but like the thief I confess to you: Remember me, O Lord, when you shall come into your kingdom. Remember me, O Master, when you shall come into your kingdom. Remember me, O Holy One, when you shall come into your kingdom. May the partaking of your Holy Mysteries, O Lord, be not for my judgment or condemnation, but for the healing of soul and body. O Lord, I also believe and profess that this, which I am about to receive, is truly your most precious Body and your life-giving Blood, which, I pray, make me worthy to receive for the remission of all my sins and for life everlasting. Amen

Appendix C:
Suggested Prayers in Thanksgiving for
The Holy Sacrifice of the Mass

Prayer of St. Thomas Aquinas (1225-1274)

Lord, Father, all-powerful and ever-living God, I thank you, for even though I am a sinner, your unprofitable servant, not because of my worth but in the kindness of your mercy, you have fed me with the precious Body and Blood of your Son, our Lord Jesus Christ. I pray that this Holy Communion may bring me not condemnation and punishment, but forgiveness and salvation. May it be a helmet of faith and a shield of good will. May it purify me from evil ways and put an end to my evil passions. May it bring me charity and patience, humility and obedience, and growth in the power to do good. May it be my strong defense against all my enemies, visible and invisible, and the perfect calming of all my evil impulses, bodily and spiritual. May it unite me more closely to you, the one true God, and lead me safely through death to everlasting happiness with you. And I pray that you will lead me, a sinner, to the banquet where you, with your Son and Holy Spirit, are true and perfect light, total fulfillment, everlasting joy, gladness without end, and perfect happiness to your saints. Grant this through Christ our Lord. Amen.

Thanksgiving after Holy Communion

My good Jesus, I pray you to bless me; keep me in your love; grant me the grace of final perseverance. Help me to become a saint. Safeguarded by you in soul and in body, may I never swerve from the right road, but surely reach your kingdom, where—not in dim mysteries, as in this dark world of ours, but—face to face we shall look upon you. There will you satisfy me with yourself and fill me with such sweetness that I shall neither hunger nor thirst forevermore: who with God the Father and the Holy Spirit lives and reigns world without end. Amen.

Prayer to St. Michael, the Archangel

St. Michael the Archangel, defend us in battle; be our protection against the wickedness and snares of the devil. May God rebuke him, we humbly pray, and do thou, O Prince of the heavenly host, by the power of God, cast into hell satan, and all the evil spirits, who wander throughout the world seeking the ruin of souls. Amen.

Prayer of Self-Dedication to Jesus Christ

Lord Jesus Christ, take all my freedom, my memory, my understanding, and my will. All that I have and cherish you have given me. I surrender it all to be guided by your will. Your grace and your love are wealth enough for me. Give me these, Lord Jesus, and I ask for nothing more.

Prayer of John Henry Cardinal Newman (1801-1890)

Dear Jesus, help us to spread your fragrance everywhere we go. Flood our souls with your spirit and life. Penetrate and possess our whole being so utterly, that our lives may be only a radiance of yours. Shine through us, and be so in us, that every soul we come in contact may feel your presence in our soul. Let them look up and see no longer us but only Jesus! Stay with us, and then we shall begin to shine as you shine; so to shine as to be a light to others; the light, O Jesus, will be all from you; none of it will be ours; it will be you, shining on others through us. Let us thus praise you in the way you love best by shining on those around us. Let us preach you without preaching, not by words but by our example, by the catching force, the sympathetic influence of what we do, the evident fullness of the love our hearts bear to you. Amen.

Appendix D:
Suggested Prayer for Receiving a "Spiritual Communion"

Prayer of St. Alphonsus Liguouri (1696-1787)

My Jesus, I believe that You are present in the Most Holy Sacrament. I love You above all things, and I desire to receive You into my soul. Since I cannot at this moment receive You sacramentally, come at least spiritually into my heart. I embrace You as if You were already there and unite myself wholly to You. Never permit me to be separated from You.

Suggested Bibliography

PAPAL ENCYCLICALS/ CONCILIAR DOCUMENTS

1. Pope Pius XII, Mediator Dei (Boston: St. Paul Books and Media, 1947).
2. Sacrosanctum Concilium (Constitution on the Sacred Liturgy, Promulgated by Pope Paul VI, 4 December 1963).
3. Pope John Paul II, Ecclesia de Eucharistia (Boston: St. Paul Books and Media, 2003).
4. Pope John Paul II, Dies Domini (Boston: St. Paul Books and Media, 1998).
5. Pope John Paul II, Mane Nobiscum Domine (New Hope, Kentucky: New Hope Publications, 2004).
6. Redemptionis Sacramentum (Washington, DC: United States Conference of Catholic Bishops, 2004).

On the Mass and the Holy Eucharist

7. Catechism of the Catholic Church (Libreria Editrice Vaticana: 2nd Edition, 1997), ¶1322-1419.
8. General Instruction of the Roman Missal, (Washington, DC: United States Conference of Catholic Bishops, 2003).
9. Belmonte, Charles Understanding the Mass (Princeton: Scepter Publishers, 1989)
10. Trese, Leo J. The Faith Explained, Third Edition (Princeton: Scepter Publishers, 2001) 347-431.
11. Elliott, Peter J. Ceremonies of the Liturgical Year (San Francisco: Ignatius Press, 2002).
12. Elliott, Peter J. Ceremonies of the Modern Roman Rite (San Francisco: Ignatius Press, 1995).
13. Elliott, Peter J. Liturgical Question Box (San Francisco: Ignatius Press, 1998).
14. Von Speyr, Adrienne. The Holy Mass (San Francisco: Ignatius Press, 1999).

Mystical/Spiritual/Philosophical Considerations of the Mass

15. Ratzinger, Joseph Cardinal The Spirit of the Liturgy (San Francisco: Ignatius Press, 2000).

16. Ratzinger, Joseph Cardinal God Is Near Us: The Eucharist, The Heart of Life (San Francisco: Ignatius Press, 2003).

17. Lang, David P. Why Matter Matters (Huntington, IN: Our Sunday Visitor, 2002).

18. Hahn, Scott The Lamb's Supper:The Mass as Heaven on Earth (New York: Doubleday, 1999).